SpringerBriefs in Economics

More information about this series at http://www.springer.com/series/8876

Andrzej K. Koźmiński • Adam Noga
Katarzyna Piotrowska • Krzysztof Zagórski

The Balanced Development Index for Europe's OECD Countries, 1999–2017

Springer

Andrzej K. Koźmiński
Kozminski University
Warsaw, Poland

Katarzyna Piotrowska
Kozminski University
Warsaw, Poland

Adam Noga
Kozminski University
Warsaw, Poland

Krzysztof Zagórski
Kozminski University
Warsaw, Poland

ISSN 2191-5504 ISSN 2191-5512 (electronic)
SpringerBriefs in Economics
ISBN 978-3-030-39239-0 ISBN 978-3-030-39240-6 (eBook)
https://doi.org/10.1007/978-3-030-39240-6

This Springer imprint is published by the registered company Springer Nature Switzerland AG
The registered company address is: Gewerbestrasse 11, 6330 Cham, Switzerland

Preface

The research project presented in this book was born out of interdisciplinary cooperation between representatives of Economics, Sociology, Management, and Statistics. The first step was modest and not very original: following the "beyond GDP paradigm," we embarked on the path of building a complex, composite index of socioeconomic well-being for one country: Poland. We produced the Balanced Development Index (BDI) tinkering with bits and pieces of knowledge drawn from different scientific disciplines.

New, more original questions emerged when we decided to use our index retroactively and to follow and explain its dynamics – that's how the idea of harmony or balance between different aspects (dimensions) of development imposed itself. Firstly, we asked ourselves a question – can BDI dynamics help to explain the logic of a business cycle? Questions about business cycle-related socioeconomic policies and their dependence on equilibrium level followed. The application of our concept and analytical tool on Poland proved encouraging.

We decided then to apply our index to 22 European members of the OECD and the EU (in the years 1999–2017) and to compare the results on the grounds of a common statistical data basis. Our sample is composed of relatively rich, economically developed democratic countries, open and exposed to global competition, all belonging to the European family of cultures and traditions. At the same time, however, our sample is highly heterogeneous, taking the level of economic development, entrenchment of democratic traditions and institutions, recent history (some of them emerged at different times from authoritarian regimes: communism and fascism), and positioning in the global networks. Such diversity calls for a comparative analysis of data. Comparisons enabled us to identify four different types of policy orientations on a country level and to point out factors propelling movements from one category to another. The results are presented below.

Since 2012, this project was graciously hosted and supported by the Interdisciplinary Center at Kozminski University. It was financed by the Kozminski University Research Fund. Our thanks go to Rector Professor Witold Bielecki and Vice Rector for Research Professor Robert Rządca for their understanding of our unorthodox ideas and generous support. We are also grateful to Sergei Druchin, our research assistant, and Agata Stepien, our administrative assistant, who helped to organize our countless meetings.

Warsaw, Poland
September 2019

Andrzej K. Koźmiński
Adam Noga
Katarzyna Piotrowska
Krzysztof Zagórski

Introduction

Europe is entering a new era, which can be referred to as "post-enlightenment" or even "post-rational." For several decades after World War II, rebuilding and consolidation efforts were guided by GDP growth-centered rationality. The problem of subjectivity and emotions has been underestimated in economic theory and overlooked in practice. At present, people are not that much after bread and butter, brick and mortar any more. They are increasingly inspired by values such as "happiness," "satisfaction," "dignity," "identity," "sovereignty," "equality," "justice," and "progress," whatever they mean by them. Emotions associated with such values, often skillfully manipulated by political hidden persuaders, have a direct impact on economic life, shaping consumption aspirations and economic behavior.

Our message from comparing 22 European OECD and EU member countries is that emotions are not good economic advice and not socially beneficial either. Following blindly people's emotional desires through increased social spending, disregarding productivity, leads nowhere. Countries immersed in emotional policies have a lower investment rate and grim prospects for the future. They tend to become dependent upon volatile international business and financial environments financing such policies at the end of the day. Reforms are needed to move from emotional to rational policies and from dependence to real sovereignty. Rational and independent countries are tempted by populist politics to move to the emotional side. They need safeguards and further reforms solidifying a rational stance and promoting socio-economic equilibrium. Otherwise, a descent toward emotional and dependent corner is inevitable. However, ignoring or underestimating the effects of public evaluations and emotions leads nowhere as well, because it strips decision-makers of necessary public and political support.

GDP is not a sufficient indicator of economic success or failure, predominantly because it doesn't take social conditions and effects into account. This is especially apparent when emotions are on the rise. A much more complex view "beyond GDP" is needed both in economic theory and practice.

This book goes much further than "beyond GDP" paradigm. It is built around the Balanced Development Index (BDI) – a composite index measuring 45 different dimensions of human and economic conditions with equal weight attached to "hard" and "soft" economic and social factors. It is not only the most complex measure of socioeconomic development but can also serve as a measure of functional equilibrium of complex socioeconomic systems and their capability to adjust to the rhythm of business and political cycle or to change it through a combination of policies. The economy of the future should essentially be interdisciplinary (sociopolitical and psychological). The BDI is intended as one of its instruments.

In the times of turbulence and generalized uncertainty, people turn to economists for clues to identify the nature of shifts and shocks, to explain the reasons and origins of the unknown, to predict the future, and to build adequate responses or strategies. In vain, mainstream economics fail in a time of crisis, when it is the most needed. As chief economic commentator at the *Financial Times* Martin Wolf (2014: 195–196) puts it: "*The economics that dominated academe and has shaped thinking for several decades proved useless in predicting, tackling or even imagining the biggest financial debacle in the world's most advanced economies for eighty years.*" World-renowned experts, practitioners, and theorists agree that oversimplifying the approach to individual and collective human actions is responsible for the failure of economics. Richard Bookstaber (2017: 13) points out that "*Expecting rationality, casting the world in a form that is amenable to mathematical and deductive methods while treating humans as mechanistic processes, will continue to fail when crises hit. And it might also fail in subtle and unapparent ways beyond the periods of crisis. But what can replace it?*" A much broader, interdisciplinary approach is needed, and that's what the BDI is all about.

A growing interest in composite measures of socioeconomic development has been present for many years. This interest stems from criticism of GDP or GNP as the indices which supposedly measure that development, while they only concern its economic side. This book presents a new Balanced Development Index (BDI), measuring the socioeconomic development in 22 European OECD and EU member countries, i.e., the democracies belonging to the globalized developed world. The BDI compares the levels and the changes in broadly understood development in these countries. In democracies, policies result from a capricious, almost random combination of external and internal, not only economic but also sociopolitical pressures, fueled by changeable, mostly emotional public moods. Economists staring at their mathematical models of GDP changes have serious problems in understanding such a world. Sociologists and political scientists, in turn, underestimate hard economic reality. A combination of subjective and objective, economic, social, psychological, and political approaches is needed to overcome these difficulties.

The equal treatment of social and economic, as well as objective and subjective, aspects of development is integral to the BDI. While our departing point was in the "beyond GDP" paradigm, which we try to develop further on, we are not taking the stance "apart from GDP," since GDP is one of the economic indicators contributing to our index. The 45 detailed indicators are aggregated into 4 composite middle-level indices: external economic (characterizing the functioning of national economies in their global, international surroundings), internal economic (characterizing domestic aspects of the economy), social expectations (concerning public and business predictions), and current social condition (including both objective and subjective social indicators). These four middle-level indices are subsequently aggregated into the general BDI. The analysis firstly concerns ranking 22 countries according to the BDI and GDP, changes in BDI levels in 1999–2017, and relations between the four aspects of socioeconomic development. Additionally, the BDI is compared with some other indices of well-being, and its changes are analyzed in relation to political changes. Conclusions emphasize the significance of social expectations and evaluations, as well as the balance between developmental aspects for available policy options. The developed economies of contemporary Europe are, to a great extent, emotional and political. The time span of our analysis enables to follow the dynamics of the index and its components. The degree of emotionality and rationality of the studied countries may vary over time.

Chapter 1 summarizes the discussions of GDP shortcomings and briefly presents various alternative approaches to measure socioeconomic development or human development, such as the Human Development Index, Human Progress Index, World Happiness Index, and quality-of-life measures. The fact that GDP simplifies a picture of economic performance and does not take social aspects of development into consideration is emphasized. A brief overview of various attempts to create alternative, more comprehensive measures of economic and social conditions suggests that these attempts result in theoretical concepts and composite measures concentrating the attention on social aspects of development but usually neglecting the economic side of it. Our Balanced Development Index (BDI) is unique because it embraces both aspects as equally important. Consecutively, chapter 1 presents a theoretical and conceptual basis of the BDI.

We do distinguish between "deductive" ("top-down" or "theory to research") and "inductive" ("bottom-up" or "research to theory") approaches. Our preference bends toward the second approach, since we appreciate the importance of empirical studies for building up or modifying the theory.

We do present four sets of detailed indicators attributed to four domains of socioeconomic development. Two of them concern the economy (its internal condition and external condition, i.e., functioning in international surrounding). Two remaining domains include current social conditions and social expectations. We emphasize an equal importance of these four domains of socioeconomic development. The BDI is constructed as an unweighted mean of composite indices of these four domains (middle-level indices). Arguments for and against weighting components of composite indices in international comparative and dynamic analyses are discussed. We have decided not to weigh detailed indicators and composite middle-level indices contributing to the BDI for both theoretical and purely statistical reasons.

To wrap up the first chapter, the relationship between socioeconomic balance and development is discussed, stressing the importance of an "optimum imbalance" to ideal equilibrium. The optimum imbalance is found to be beneficial for the development and the most appropriate situation for pro-developmental reforms. Both a high imbalance and an almost perfect balance inhibit development.

Chapter 2 shows international differences in the level and pace of socioeconomic development, as measured by the BDI. It also compares rankings by the BDI and

Table 1 Four types of a country's economies

	Rationality – emotionality	
Independency-dependency	Independent, rational	Independent, emotional
	Dependent, rational	Dependent, emotional

GDP per capita. While these two indices are – of course – positively correlated, there are interesting differences between them in different countries and periods. The chapter begins with analyses of the changes in the BDI and its four composite components in European OECD member countries. A special emphasis is given to distinguish pre-crisis, crisis, and post-crisis periods. The groups of more and less developed countries are also compared. The chapter also discusses the correlations between the BDI and social conditions measured by such indices as the Human Development Index, Human Progress Index, and World Happiness index. The main assumption is that the final aim of socioeconomic development is not economic growth but human well-being and "flourishing." The BDI analysis opens the space for policy debate.

Through the combination of two axes, dependent vs. independent countries and rational vs. emotional ones, four types of countries are identified: independent emotional, dependent emotional, independent rational, and dependent rational (Table 1).

All four groups are briefly discussed. Longitudinal analysis spanned over time enables countries moving from one category to another to be identified. It opens the space for analysis of reforms. Unfortunately, the time span 1999–2017 is not long enough for more solidly grounded theoretical conclusions.

Chapter 3 presents three cases of successful and unsuccessful reforms aimed at rationalizing economies hit by the crisis: Germany, Greece, and Spain.

Chapter 4 contains an in-depth case study of socioeconomic development in Poland – a country in which the BDI was first conceived and applied. This case study is particularly interesting since Poland was the only European country not affected by the last financial crisis as measured by GDP but where the BDI indicated a substantive effect of this crisis on comprehensively measured socioeconomic conditions. Poland is the only dependent rational country in our sample. It appears as a transition economy in 1989 lagging behind even some of its "socialist" peers from Central Europe and unexpectedly transformed into a global growth champion (Piatkowski 2018) but paying price for it in terms of social relations.

Chapter 5 is devoted to conclusions related to BDI as a tool of economic and policy analysis. Our analysis demonstrates that it is difficult to project the BDI into the future. Nevertheless, it helps to develop scenarios for the future based on the finding that development is hampered by both an extreme balance (equilibrium) and an extreme imbalance (disequilibrium) and instigated by a moderate imbalance. The distinction and measurement of such four aspects of socioeconomic development as internal economic, external economic, current social conditions, and social expectations appeared very useful for analyzing socioeconomic development in various countries. Mainstream economics, both before and after the crisis of 2007–2013, did not include an analysis of emotionally driven social expectations and a functional balance and system control. These are the topics tackled within our BDI analysis Such research fields host theoretical disputes about the identification of the mechanism of the business cycle and instruments of its correction.

When it comes to policy implications, the message from BDI analysis turns our attention toward people's subjective perceptions, expectations, and emotions fueling political processes. The level of socioeconomic balance directs and constrains future policies. It should be monitored, if policy-makers are to maintain a sufficient level of political support, while implementing development programs. When policies become predominantly shaped by people's emotions and desires (mostly expressed in different kinds of social welfare programs), countervailing rational programs like Hartz-Schröder's German reforms is needed. This calls for a well-orchestrated political support probably more difficult to obtain than in the case of populist programs. Systematically updating the BDI might be helpful in building up such political support. A future research agenda can be built around these theoretical and practical issues.

In a nut shell, the conclusions of our analysis are the following:

1. The BDI, designed and applied for 22 European members of the OECD and the EU, has some unique characteristics. Firstly, it measures well-being in the most complex way, embracing social and economic factors on equal grounds. Secondly, it measures the level of socioeconomic equilibrium, describing phases of the business cycle in the most complex way. Thirdly, it indicates social expectations and provides insight into their role in business cycle dynamics.
2. The BDI and its four middle-level components (internal economic, external economic, current social conditions, and social expectations) are useful in analyzing socioeconomic development in various countries. We have found that "post-World War II modern era of enlightenment" in the most advanced European countries seems to be coming to an end. Europe is swinging between rationality and emotionality. If traps set by emotional policies are to be avoided, a broad-minded interdisciplinary analysis of socioeconomic equilibrium is needed. And that's what the BDI is all about.
3. People's emotions, subjective assessments of current situations, and hopes for the future subvert and modify purely economic mechanisms. The real economy is becoming increasingly social and political and by the same token more unpredictable on the ground of a conventional economic analysis.
4. Neither mainstream economics and social sciences nor generally practiced policies are helpful in understanding and mastering the complex socioeconomic situation. The BDI analysis can help to grapple and to alternate new "socialized" business cycles and development processes, to some extent.

Contents

Chapter 1
BDI: A New Measure of Well-Being and Governability

1 GDP Shortcomings and the New Approaches

Until the second half of the twentieth century, socio-economic development was almost exclusively identified with and measured by Gross Domestic Product or Net Domestic Product, despite the shortcomings of both these concepts. Simon Kuznets (1934), forefather of national accounts and Nobel Prize winner in economics, stressed more than 80 years ago that GDP is too simplistic to characterize the economy and its development, let alone both economic and social aspects of development together. About a quarter of century later, an extension of this critical opinion came from John Galbraith (1958), another prominent economist. Recently, a brief but comprehensive summary of GDP shortcomings and related problems was presented in a report by the Commission on the Measurement of Economic Performance and Social Progress (Stiglitz et al. 2010: 23–59). The initial presumption directing the Commission's work was that irrespective of the conceptual and technical shortcomings of the GDP, the overemphasizing importance of production and supply of goods and services stems from confusing means of socio-economic development with its goals, which should be broadly understood as the general (not only material) well-being of people.

Despite early criticism by paramount economists and despite the growing consciousness of GDP limitations, serious work on its supplementing, or replacing started not earlier than around 50 years ago, stimulated by an interest in social indicators (Bauer 1966; Cohen 1968; Sheldon and Moore 1968; Drewnowski 1970; Moser 1970, 1973; Galtung 1976; UNESCO 1976; Fox 1977; Zapf 2000; Delhey et al. 2002; Atkinson et al. 2002). The establishment of a quarterly journal "Social Indicators Research" and a Working Group for Social Indicators of the International Sociological Association constituted milestones in the development of broad international cooperation platform that was named "social indicators

A. K. Koźmiński et al., *The Balanced Development Index for Europe's OECD Countries, 1999–2017*, SpringerBriefs in Economics,
https://doi.org/10.1007/978-3-030-39240-6_1

movement". The history and comprehensive overview of theoretical, empirical and organizational issues of this movement was presented by Michalos (2014), Noll and Michalos (2014), Land and Michalos (2018).

The social indicators movement has inspired attempts to elaborate the integrated system of social and demographic statistics that emerged at the international level (UN 1975) including Poland (Zagórski 1975). Richard Stone, who received a Nobel Prize for his work on national accounts, attempted to link social and demographic statistics to these accounts and advocated construction of socio-demographic flow matrices similar to those reflecting input-output inter-industrial flows (Stone 1966, 1971). Various national social reports, social indicators reports and social statistics reports started to be published by statistical offices and other research institutions all over the world.

The social indicators movement was based on an assumption that the main aim of socio-economic development is the quality of life or well-being of people rather than economic growth which should be treated only as a condition to achieve such an aim (Allardt 1993; Diener 1995; Moser 1970; Noll 2004). That assumption remains undisputed and is widely accepted till now (Stiglitz et al. 2010), though it is still too often ignored or forgotten by too many economists and politicians.

The concepts of well-being and quality of life have been soon extended to the concept of happiness (Veenhoven 1984; Veenhoven et al. 1993). Happiness and its indicators began to be a new research field for economists and has integrated the science of economics with psychology and sociology (Easterlin 2002; Di Tella et al. 2003; Di Tella and MacCulloch 2006; Van Praag et al. 2004; Frey 2008; Frey and Stutzer 2008; Carabelli and Cedrini 2011; Frey and Gallus 2013; Veenhoven 2018).

The social indicators movement quickly led to work on composite indices of social development, with UNRISD's research program being the pioneer (McGranahan et al. 1970). After a period of inexplicable lack of interest in such endeavors, new attempts to design and apply composite indices were made by Estes and his collaborators (Estes and Morgan 1976; Estes 1984, 1988, 2019) working on the International Index of Social Progress, and by Morris (1980), who worked on the Physical Quality of Life Index. A bit later, Dienner (1995) introduced his basic and then advanced Quality of Life Indices (QOL). The initiative by King of Bhutan who inspired the Gross National Happiness index to be developed for his country is very well known. Its latest discussion was presented by Pennock and Ura (2011), and Ura et al. (2012). The number of such projects has recently been growing almost exponentially, so a presentation of their complete list is impossible (Dijkstra 2002; Cummins et al. 2003; Berenger and Verdier-Chouchane 2007; Costanza et al. 2009; NEF 2009; Schepelmann et al. 2009; Bilbao-Ubillos 2013; Espina and Arechavala 2013; Huppert and So 2013; Madonia et al. 2013; OECD 2013; Reig-Martínez 2013; UNDP 2013; Porter et al. 2015, Smits and Steendijk 2015; Ivaldi et al. 2016; Davino et al. 2018; Yifu Lin et al. 2019; Bericat and Jiménez-Rodrigo 2019, to give some examples only). In Poland, the proposal to construct a composite index of economic and social aspects of development was made by Grzegorz Kołodko (2011). The first version of our Balanced Development Index was designed following this proposal only for Poland (Koźmiński et al. 2014, 2015, 2016). Its modification and application to international comparisons constitutes the main aim of the present publication.

The discussion initiated by Stiglitz and co-authors is still going on around the question whether to construct composite indices or rather to apply a "dashboard approach" i.e. a carefully selected set of simple indicators (Fleurbayey and Blanchet 2013: 27–33). Fleurbayey and Blanched expressed the opinion that several "middle-level" composite indices may measure various aspects of social conditions better than the sets of simple indicators

All-in-all, the social indicators movement has nowadays evolved into a wide, meandering and rocky stream of conceptual work and research "Beyond GDP" (Fleurbaey and Blanchet 2013; Stiglitz et al. 2010, 2018a, b). The construction of various quality-of-life composite indices remains in the mainstream of this research together with attempts to design various comprehensive dashboards of indicators (for a discussion see: Hagerty et al. 2001; Sirgy 2011; Fleurbaey and Blanchet 2013; Bericat and Jiménez-Rodrigo 2019).

In addition to the UN (particularly UNDP) and OECD, various state authorities have also expressed a rapidly growing interest in complex country-specific measures of socio-economic development. The program commissioned by French President Nicolas Sarkozy (Stiglitz et al. 2010) should be mentioned in first order, but there were also programs initiated by the German Bundestag (Giesselmann et al. 2013) and the Italian parliament (BES 2014). Our index of balanced socio-economic development (BDI) for Poland was presented in 2014 at a conference organized by Polish President Bronisław Komorowski. The last economic crisis produced growing interest in a complex approach to development, with an emphasis on people's well-being (Guardiola et al. 2014; Arechavala et al. 2015). Further development of the project initiated by President Sarkozy takes place under OECD auspices (Stiglitz et al. 2018a, b). Though the priority of this project is to construct comprehensive dashboards of single indicators of the most important aspects of social and economic conditions, the authors adhere to their initial opinion that a well-designed list of indicators should allow for the aggregation of all or some of them into more general composite indices according to researchers' different needs and philosophies (Stiglitz et al. 2010: 12–13).

It is worth noting that long-lasting research, which evolved from the "social indicators movement" to "beyond GDP" projects, have gradually been attracting interest and then instigating actions of politicians rather than other way around. Though composite socio-economic indices are still rarely used in policy formulations, we believe that the work on various dashboards of indicators has not only intensified but also prompted such actions as setting United Nations' "Millennium Development Goals – MDGs" and then "Sustainable Development Goals – SDGs" (for a brief discussion see: Kanbur et al. 2018: 33–48). In order to monitor the fulfilment of these goals, particular indicators have been designed for each of them. The subsequent approval of MDGs by 150 world leaders at the Millennium Summit in 2000 and SDGs by the UN General Assembly in 2015 have made them official and contributed to the real improvement of social and economic conditions or at least to the better measurement of them in many countries around the world. Of course, it is difficult to say how important this contribution was, since the progress depends on very many things.

Some of the projects mentioned above concern only social indicators, while others combine social and economic ones. However, even those not totally neglecting the economy tend to overemphasize social aspects and underemphasize economic aspects of development. SDGs place a larger emphasis on economic aspects than the earlier MDGs, so the trend is in heading in a good direction, at least. Our Balanced Development Index goes further, since it treats economic and social aspects as equally important.

The question arises whether composite indices of social well-being or socio-economic development rank countries much differently from the Gross National Product. Our comparison concerns European OECD member countries and three often used indices of better life, human development and world happiness.

The *Better Life Index*, elaborated and published by the OECD (2017) is a two-tier dashboard of indicators grouped in 11 domains, such as: housing, income (more precisely material living conditions), jobs, community and social network, education, environment, civic engagement, health, life satisfaction, safety and work-life balance. Each of these domains is described by a few detailed statistical indicators which are compressed into 11 middle-level indices. The OECD does not compute and publish its own general index of better life. Instead, it provides an open access computerized system without any restrictions that allows each user, being an individual or institution, to assign preferred weight to each middle-level index and to calculate a general index as a mean of such weighted domains for each country. This is fully consistent with the already mentioned Stiglitz, Fleurbaey and their co-authors' stance that particular social and economic indicators should be aggregated into higher level indices adequately to different researchers' needs, preferences, values and theoretical approaches. Here, we assign equal weights to each domains, an approach that will be explained later on.

The *Human Development Index*, elaborated and published by the United Nations (UNDP 2018), consists of three domains: the ability to lead a long and healthy life, the ability to acquire knowledge and the ability to achieve a decent standard of living. The latest is measured by GDP per capita, and the economic aspect of development is as important as health and education. The UNDP publishes a general HDI index.

The *World Happiness Index*, elaborated and published by the Sustainable Development Solutions Network (Helliwell et al. 2018), presents national means of peoples' satisfactions from 11 domains of life: personal relationships, main activity or occupation, personal achievements, health, future expectations, standard of life, neighborhood, leisure time, city, countryside and citizen security. World Happiness Index differs from two other indices, since all its constituting indicators are subjective and they are collected by Gallup Poll's representative sociological surveys.

It is evident that despite the differences in their composition all three socio-economic indices somehow overlap thematically and one of them even includes GDP among its components. Since the main motive of their design was to

Table 1.1 Ranking of 22 OECD European countries by different socio-economic development indices, 2017

Gross Domestic Product	Better Life Index	Human Development Index	World Happiness Index
1. Luxembourg	**1. Denmark**	**1. Ireland**	**1 Finland**
2. Ireland	**2. Sweden**	**2. Germany**	**2 Denmark**
3. Netherlands	**3. Finland**	**3. Sweden**	3 Netherlands
4. Sweden	4. Netherlands	4. Netherlands	4 Sweden
5. Denmark	**5. Belgium**	5. Denmark	**5. Austria**
6. Austria	**6. Germany**	**6. United Kingdom**	6 Ireland
7. Germany	7. Luxembourg	**7. Finland**	7. Germany
8. Belgium	8. Ireland	8. Belgium	8. Belgium
9. Finland	**9.United Kingdom**	9. Austria	9. Luxembourg
10. United Kingdom	10. Austria	10. Luxembourg	10. United Kingdom
11. France	11. France	11. France	**11. Czech Republic**
12. Italy	**12. Spain**	**12. Slovenia**	12. France
13. Spain	**13. Slovenia**	13. Spain	13. Spain
14. Czech Republic	14. Czech Republic	14. Czech Republic	**14. Slovakia**
15. Slovenia	**15. Estonia**	15. Italy	**15. Poland**
16. Slovakia	16. Italy	**16. Estonia**	16. Italy
17. Estonia	17. Slovakia	**17. Greece**	17. Slovenia
18. Portugal	**18. Poland**	**18. Poland**	**18. Latvia**
19. Poland	19. Portugal	19. Slovakia	19. Estonia
20. Hungary	**20. Latvia**	20. Portugal	20. Hungary
21. Latvia	21. Hungary	21. Latvia	21 Portugal
22. Greece	22.Greece	22.Hungary	22 Greece

Note: Countries higher in rankings by particular indices than by GDP are printed in bold

provide more comprehensive and – more importantly – a more socially oriented measure than GDP, it is reasonable to check, how differently than GDP they rank countries and how all four rankings differ from each other. As already said, we will concentrate on 22 European OECD member countries. For the sake of simplicity, we will compare four rankings in one year only (Table 1.1).

There is a group of countries which occupy high places in all four rankings, though their detailed sequences somehow vary. These are: Ireland, Netherlands, Sweden, Denmark and Finland – the highly developed welfare countries together with Ireland experiencing spectacular growth even sometimes called "the Irish miracle". There is also a group of countries located low in all rankings, namely: Greece, Hungary, Latvia and Portugal – all relatively small countries that much suffered from last economic crisis strengthened by particular domestic circumstances. Despite differences in the strength of their economy, much larger France and Spain take similar places in all four rankings, close do the middle. Some countries are characterized by significant discrepancies. Luxembourg is a small country with the highest GDP but takes only between 7th and 10th place on the three remaining indices. Italy takes 12th place in respect of GDP but 15th–16th place in the three other

Table 1.2 Correlations between different socio-economic development indices of 22 European countries, 2017

	Human development index	World happiness index	GDP	Mean correlation
Better life index	.909	.930	.895	.911
Human development index		.860	.887	.885
World happiness index			.872	.887
GDP				.885

Note: All correlations significant at .01 level

rankings. On the other hand, Poland is only 19th as far as GDP is concerned, but 15th in terms of happiness.

However, all ranking differences look a bit chaotic and difficult to interpret. They depend on very particular configurations of simple indicators contributing to the different indices. The similarity between different rankings may be best assessed by their correlations.

Consistent with possible expectations, Table 1.2 shows quite high correlations between all indices, GDP included. There are exceptionally high, almost perfect correlations between the Better Life Index, Human Development Index and World Happiness Index. They are correlated between each other at the level of about .90. Such strong correlations are very rarely seen in social sciences. The correlations between them and GDP are lower but negligibly. Thus, despite declared substantive and substantial differences, all three indices yield very similar results, if applied to Western and Central European countries at least. The question still remains to be answered, how sensible is the use of various social or socio-economic indices which are highly correlated with GDP or other measures of wealth. Dienner and Such (1997) have found a very high correlation between the QOL Index and per capita purchasing power of the nations, even higher than the correlations between GDP and the three indices presented in Table 1.2. However, they have pointed out several outlier countries, some much better and some much worse in terms of QOL than it could have been expected because of their economic performance. Similar discrepancies appear in comparing our rankings by GDP and other indices. We have already mentioned Luxembourg, but this is a very specific small town-country. Denmark may serve as a more interesting example of discrepancy, being much higher in terms of Better Life and World Happiness indices than in terms of GDP. There are several other examples of such discrepancies. Thus, we fully agree with Diener and Suh (1997: 193) that "*…strong correlations between economic indicators and social indicators do not suggest that the latter are not needed. Quite the contrary, one value of social indicators is that they contain information beyond that which is contained in economic measures*". Moreover, widely accepted statistical assumptions are that the composite index, though losing some detailed information, is a better, more reliable and robust measure of a general concept than a set of separate indicators.

All that leads to the conclusion that an index is needed which will measure both economic (wealth) and social (quality of life) aspects together, but which will allow its disaggregation into economic and social domains. As already stated, there are four such domains in our case: external economic conditions, internal economic conditions, current social conditions and social expectations. Several detailed indicators, aggregated into four middle-level indices, describe all these domains.

2 Conceptual and Theoretical Grounds of BDI

The BDI is essentially different from other composite indices proposed in the past. Firstly, because it is more complex and provides better insights into interrelated social and economic aspects of well-being. Second, because it allows dynamic controllability of socio-economic systems to be assessed and has clear policy implications.

The strategic dilemma we have faced designing our research is whether social scientists should try to build-up and empirically driven theories understood as sets of interrelated generalizations (Carnap 1962; Dillard 1948) or rather to conduct theory driven (inspired) empirical research (Popper 1959). This is one of the basic dilemmas in the social sciences. It can be understood as inductive versus the deductive knowledge cumulation process (Nowak 1977) or bottom-up versus top-down proceeding (Sirgy 2011: 7–8). We are inclined to follow the first rather than the second approach, but not pushed to the extreme. Some theoretical framework is always useful to layout grounds for further empirical research: to develop basic concepts and hypothesis or at least to formulate research issues or questions to be answered empirically. Such a theoretical framework does not have to come from one theory, one school of thought or even one discipline of science. It can be eclectic, using categories from different sources embracing different key aspects of researched reality. Empirical research should contribute to modifying, or at least developing theories from which initial concepts stem from.

Such a methodological approach generates a research–theory cycle enriching both in a sequence of iterations rather than having one influence the other in a predetermined one way direction. We do not adopt any single comprehensive general theory coming from one discipline of the social sciences as a blueprint for our project. Our analyses are conducted in search of regularities in the form of historical generalizations that may have some more general theoretical implications (Malewski 1962) in several disciplines of the social sciences (Fig. 1.1).

Our credo is interdisciplinarity. As shown above, we are inspired by the shortcomings of composite well-being indices falling into the category of "beyond GDP" indicators which neglect the economic side of development. When designing the BDI, we are driven by the idea of balance between social and economic dimensions of countries' development. Economic and sociological concepts were prime sources of inspiration. Possible conclusions concerning the ability of managing development came out later as a consequence of embracing tensions between

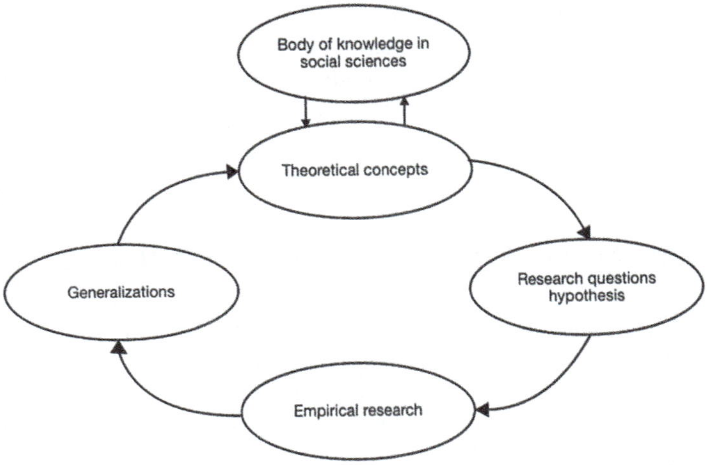

Fig. 1.1 Research-theory cycle

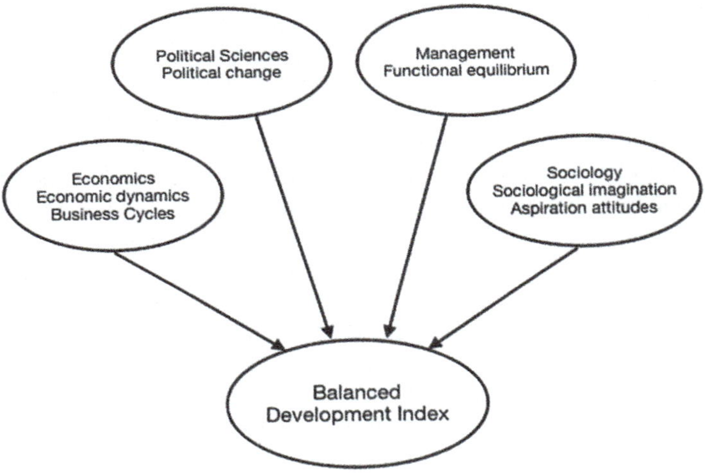

Fig. 1.2 Conceptual grounds of the BDI

social and economic, "soft" and "hard" factors and took us towards management concepts (Fig. 1.2).

Michał Kalecki (1943a, b) was the pioneer of business cycles analysis concerning both economic and social factors. His theory of "political cycle" is focused almost exclusively on tensions between capital and labor, or, in other words: class conflict. In contemporary economic analysis, the Marxist idea of class conflict is replaced by income inequality and quality of life differences as sources of dysfunctional tensions. Neo-Marxists and Neo-Keynesians (Atkinson and Piketty 2010; Atkinson 2015) are adherent to this line of thought. It is also embraced by an emerging, new eclectic pragmatism in economics (Kołodko 2017). Under such influence, variables related to social inequalities were included in the BDI.

Behavioral economics pushed us towards the emotional side of economic choices: confidence and its multipliers, expectations of the future situation, hopes and fears, subjective perception of economic and social life (Akerloff and Shiller 2010). Behavioral economics and a modern neo classical analysis embrace economic actors' expectations: rational, adaptive, extrapolative, explorative and irrational ("animal instincts"). They were translated into sociological indicators and included in the BDI. Such an understanding of the social and emotional side of the business cycle was also influenced by the "Economics of Happiness" school of thought and the category of "experienced utility", understood in hedonistic terms as general satisfaction and a feeling of happiness linked to the perception of individual and collective economic situation (Di Tella et al. 2003; Di Tella and MacCulloch 2006; Frey 2008; Brulé and Suter 2019). An inquiry into the emotional side of economic life opens another line of thinking about the dynamics of socio-economic systems: the macroeconomics of populism developed by Dornbush and Edwards (1989) on the grounds of in-depth studies of Latin American countries in the 1970s. These ideas seem particularly valid when confronted with recent political ("new nationalism") and economic ("new protectionism") developments around the world.

The complexity of BDI as a measurement tool calls for the inclusion of typical "hard" indicators as "real business cycle" theories stipulate (Kydland and Prescott 1982). That's why indicators of GDP growth, employment, inflation, cost of money etc. make up an important part of the BDI. In a globalized and open economy, the competitive advantage any given country enjoys as well as its chances of sustainable growth and development depend upon external relations with the international economic environment. This is one of the few unquestioned axioms of economics (Porter 1990; Barro and Martin 2003; Landels 2015). As a result, such standard indicators as: import, export, exchange rate, FDI or interest on government debt etc. had to be included.

The sociological inspiration of the BDI research is quite obvious. It comes from the well-known concept of well-being. That's why an extended portfolio of social indicators (such as: welfare, education, R&D, health care expenditures, crime rates, infant mortality, homicides etc.) is included. It sums up to time series of snap shots presenting the current social situation in surveyed countries and it offers a sense of dynamics. Understanding, however, and transposing the picture of reality into the future is more important than the picture itself. In this respect we were inspired by C.W. Mills's (1959) concept of "sociological imagination". In such a framework attitudes, emotions, hopes and fears are brought into the picture contributing to the system's controllability its proneness to be subject to governance and policies, and eventually to structural reforms, aimed at the "competitive advantage of nations" as Michael Porter (1990) calls it.

Political science explains mechanisms of power conditioning governance processes, policies and reforms, in particular. Power is driven, diverted and often blocked (Naim 2013) by people's emotions, attitudes and opinions. In what way? On the most general level, an explanation is offered by general systems and

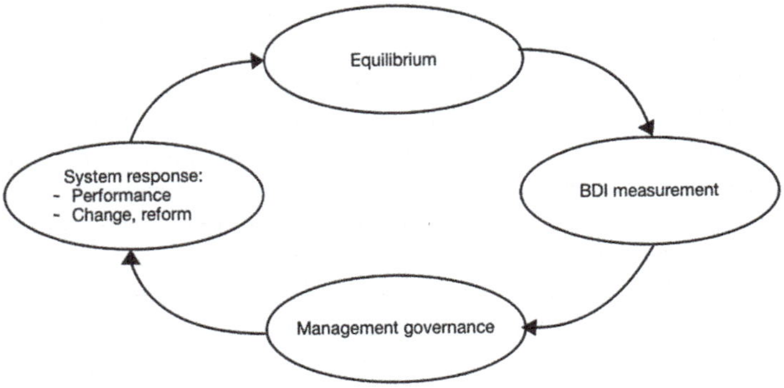

Fig. 1.3 BDI as equilibrium measure

general equilibrium theory (Weintraub 1974; Lapunov 1992). On the management (governance) level (Kaplan and Norton 1996; Cavaleri and Obloj 1993) the message is simple: equilibrium is manageable through preconditioning controllability and the development of the socio-economic system. In order to manage equilibrium one has to measure it. The BDI is the unique tool enabling such measurement (Fig. 1.3).

Greco et al. (2019) have proved on the example of more than 400 different composite indices that their authors apply very different approaches in the selection, aggregation and weighting of simple indicators (index components). Diagnostic, explanatory and predictive values of indicators may differ depending on different goals of the analysis. Moreover, they may change in time and differ in different socio-economic contexts. Thus, a large list of simple indicators makes them useful from more than one point of view and makes the index more universal. That is one of the main assumptions of our project, since we are interested not only in the dynamics of generally defined development, but – to a greater extent – in relative dynamics of its four domains: external economic, internal economic, current social and social expectations. The interrelations between four of them are often more interesting than the generalized level of development. Of course, the latter is important as well. However, changes of indicators are more important for us than their level. That follows Pareto's concept of ordinal rather than cardinal utility.

Our previous analyses of the BDI and its components for Poland (Koźmiński et al. 2014, 2015, 2016), have proved a diagnostic, explanatory and predictive value of our model of socio-economic development, as consisting of four of the above-mentioned complex components. A modification of the list of simple indicators constituting the BDI may be compared to a modification of the GDP since its first design by Kuznets. Arguments about including or excluding several GDP components, constant attempts to include some new components into it, occupy a lot of space in economy handbooks and are subjects of many anecdotes and paradoxes. Changes in GDP composition and calculation are often arbitrary and abductive, though made with all "bells and whistles" of refined statistical and economic methods. Thus, the selection of index components (detailed indicators) and the problem of their weighting or not weighting seems to be cognitively very seminal, especially in the context of balanced development and governability.

All that leads to the conclusion that an index is needed which will measure both economic (wealth) and social (quality of life) aspects together, but which will allow its disaggregation into economic and social domains. As already stated, there are four such domains in our case: external economic conditions, internal economic conditions, current social conditions and social expectations. As many as 45 detailed indicators describe all these domains. They are aggregated into four middle-level indices, the rationale for the selection of which is given below.

3 Four Domains of Socio-economic Development: Selection of Indicators

The "Beyond GDP" approach is based on an assumption that a strictly economic approach to development, i.e. concentrating the attention on GDP changes, does not lead to the proper assessment of human progress and well-being. We have to take into consideration such social aspects of development as non-market and social provisions, stock and flows of physical, natural and human capital and distributional items at least (Kanbur et al. 2018: 34). Thus, both economic and social indicators are needed, especially those which are related to social progress and human well-being (Brulé and Suter 2019).

The concurrent analysis of many different economic aspects of development is based on the assumption that they may change in different pace, quite irrespectively of the possible high correlation between them. Thus for example, in condition of GDP growth by 5%, the investment may grow by either 3% or by 15%, consumption may rise by either 2% or 4%, the import by 5% or 10% or it may even decline, electricity production may remain the same or grow considerably, etc. A good example is Greece, where the discrepancy between the pace of economic growth and consumption has caused a severe crisis even in times when both of them were rising.

"The Atlas of Economic Complexity – Mapping Paths to Prosperity" constitutes an earlier valuable example of a complex description of economic changes different from GDP changes (Hausmann et al. 2013). It takes international economic exchange and economic competitiveness of enterprises and households into account. The Economic Complexity Index (ICI) constitutes its main indicator. It uses two kinds of data. The first concerns the diversity of the export from given countries, its internal structure, i.e. how much of which products is exported from a country and how competitive this country is in exporting that particular products. The second concerns ubiquity, i.e. the number of countries that export particular goods competitively. The complexity of a country's economy and its products may constitute an additional concern here. The more complex the country's economy is and the more complex its products are, the greater the chances for development on a macro (country) and micro (households) scale.

The "Atlas of Economic Complexity" includes only several indicators. Their list may be much extended in order to present a more comprehensive description of the economy. It may be useful to consider not only export, but also import, currency exchange rates, foreign investment, stock exchange, spreads between interest rates, etc. GDP may be another useful addition. The comparison of changes in GDP to changes in detailed simple indicators contributing to the BDI or to changes in its middle-level indices may reveal possible discrepancies leading to economic or social turbulence or – quite the opposite – instigate further development. That may happen when some detailed indicators or middle level indices rise slower than GDP. It may also happen that the decline of GDP in crisis times is not accompanied by a similar decline in other indicators, especially social ones. Of course, the interpretation and evaluation of such discrepancies depends on the researcher's value system and other concerns.

The selection of detailed indicators and their aggregation in middle-level indices should be based on theoretical model of socio-economic development as J. M. Keynes wrote to R. Harrod: "*Economics is science of thinking in terms of models joined to the art of choosing models which are relevant to the contemporary world. It is compelled to be this, because, unlike the typical natural science, the material to which it is applied is, in too many respects, not homogeneous through time (…). Good economist are scarce because the gift for using 'vigilant observation' to choose good models, although it does not require a highly specialized intellectual technique, appears to be a very rare one*" (Keynes, 1971: 297).

3.1 External Functioning of a Nation's Economy

We acknowledge that societies and their economies are presently functioning in a global economic context. However, we would like to avoid an acrimonious and overly ideological dispute between the advocates and the critics of globalization. Instead, we simply interpret globalization after Robertson (1992: 116) as an "intra-societal civilizing process", and we share the opinion that the impact of globalization on domestic socioeconomic conditions may vary from country to country (Lee and Vivarelli 2006) or from domain to domain. Irrespective of that, the globalization jointly concern intertwined economic and social aspects of development. Several examples are listed below:

- Dependence on foreign capital seems to have a positive effect on income inequality and population growth, but hampers economic growth, which is facilitated by the openness of markets (Kentor 2001);
- Democracy seems to be positively influenced by foreign direct investment, but negatively by portfolio investment (Li and Reuveny 2003);
- Globalization causes a need to implement international labor standards, thus improving employment conditions (Sengenberger 2002);

- The shift of industrial production from high to low labor-cost countries may have a positive effect on employment and living conditions in the latter, but negative in the former group of societies.

It is not important here to discuss how well these statements are documented by sound empirical analyses. What needs to be emphasized is the need to analyze each country's socio-economic development in its global economic context. This applies especially to transition and post-transition countries, such as: Poland, Hungary, the Czech Republic, and even more so the small Baltic states depending very much on international cooperation and exchange. The post-communist transformation to market economies is taking place at a time of globalization. Hence, integration with the world economy is an indispensable part of this transformation (Kołodko 2002: 83). Increasing foreign direct investment and opening up previously relatively closed economies make an important contribution to this process (Ibidem: 5–6). Thus, economic performance in an international context and a level of successful integration with the world economic system are no less important than the domestic aspects of the economy. We assume that various aspects of the external (international) economic situation have a significant impact of internal functioning of the economy, socio-economic development in general, functional equilibrium and governability of the system. They may influence fiscal and monetary policy, expectations concerning the profitability of investment, as well as consumption. All these may shape social expectations. We have selected seven indicators of seven different aspects of the functioning of an economy in international surroundings.

As presented in Table 1.3, our detailed indicators of the functioning of the economy in its external (international, global) context concern seven domains:

Foreign direct investments indicate professional evaluation of business capabilities in a country by international capital. This capital very seriously treats professional analyses, *due diligence* and others, by its own analysts or external consulting agencies (e.g. SWOT, VRIO, PEST, intelligence agencies). Direct foreign investors base their decisions on such professional analyses but are sometimes also the subject of bureaucratic inertia. In both cases they are not directed by strong emotional reactions to economic and political changes, so their decisions reflect relatively objective conditions. They are usually moderately correlated with GDP, so they constitute valuable additional information about the economy.
(Source of data: World Development Indicators (World Bank))

Import and export per capita constitute the most natural indicators of the international functioning of the economy, quite important for economic stability and governability. Their correlation with GDP is usually quite high. However, their changes may sometimes substantially differ from GDP changes. Import growing disproportionally to GDP and to export may result in a serious foreign trade deficit, difficult to reduce without direct foreign investment. Such a positive impact of FDI was apparent in Poland in the late 1990's. Growing export may exert a similarly positive

Table 1.3 Four domains of development and their indicators

External economic	Social expectations
Foreign direct investment Import (per capita) Export (per capita) National currency exchange rate to $ National bonds' value (spread to FRG) National bonds' value (spread to USA) Stock exchange index	Public expectation: life in general Public expectation: economic situation of a country Public expectation: financial situation of households Public expectation: employment situation on the labor market Public expectation: one's own employment situation Business expectations: tendency of production in manufacturing Business expectations: activity in retail trade
Internal economic	**Current social conditions**
GDP per capita, PPP 2010 Production of electricity Accumulation (% of GDP) Inflation rate Household final consumption Unemployment rate Public debt (% of GDP) Yearly increase in real average wages Business perception of the current activity tendency and production tendency in manufacturing Business perception of the current activity tendency in retail trade Business perception of the current activity tendency in service	Coefficient of births Coefficient of marriages Population aged 0–14 (% of the total) Infant mortality (per 1000 births) Public expenses for health service (% of GDP) Public expenses for a "welfare state" (% of GDP) GINI coefficient Consumption of energy from renewable sources (% of general energy consumption) CO_2 emission (metric tons per person) Threat of poverty (% of households) Internet access (% of households) "R&D" researcher (per one million of the population Youth unemployment Robberies (per 100,000 people) Homicides (per 100,000 people) Confidence in the government Social assessment of the country's economic situation Material evaluation of the material situation of households Social assessment of the situation on the job market.

impact. That is the rationale behind including jointly indicators of direct foreign investment, import and export among "external" economic indicators.

Information concerning export also indicates business competitiveness and allows such things as "upselling" or "monter en gamme" as suggested by P. Artus and S. Broyer (2013) to be assessed. The already mentioned authors of *The Atlas of Economic Complexity* (Hausmann et al. 2013), interpret the composition of export as indicating the level of socio-economic development and the position of the country in the world.
(Source of data: OECD)

The currency exchange rate constitutes another hard indicator of economic functioning in the international context. In addition to import and export, it contributes to a more comprehensive assessment of current trade accounts and financial flows. A high exchange rate of a particular currency in a situation of a negative balance of international trade or *vice versa* provides valuable economic information. The exchange rate is a strong correlate of economic development indicating not only the strength or weakness of exporters and importers but also the financial condition of many enterprises or households that may have debts in foreign currency. Despite of the fact that the majority of European OECD member countries use a common Euro currency we have decided to include the currency exchange rate among our indicators because of its importance for those countries that have not joined the Euro-zone.

Particular exchange rates may, however, be artificially low or high in relation to the actual condition of a nation's economy due to many factors, financial speculations among them. Such a danger of distortion can be grossly reduced by consideration of a greater number of different indicators and by aggregating them into more general indices.
(Source of data: OECD, Eurostat)

Spreads between the interest rates of country's bonds and American (US) as well as German bonds are seldom used but are a valuable measure of international confidence in a country's economy. The US and Germany enjoy high and stable confidence on a global financial market, so we have decided to use them as benchmarks. Though some nationalist doctrines consider that measure as distorting the real condition of a nation's economy, it actually constitutes a good *quick test* in a market analysis situation. In many cases, its addition to other economic indicators allows a more realistic assessment of the economy. Poland in 2018 may serve as a good example. The spreads between Polish and American as well as German bonds have been rising in Poland despite a 5% growth of GDP and halted growth of the public debt. That indicated some hidden dangers faced by the Polish economy. Thus, while not perfect indicators alone, the spreads are very good components of the composite index, when supplementing other indicators. The shortcomings of all of them cancel each other and jointly present a more realistic picture of the economy rather than cumulate and distort this picture further on.
(Source of data: Federal Reserve Bank of St. Louis)

The stock exchange index is included among the "external" factors rather than the "internal" ones, owing to a huge dependence on foreign investors in most cases. Similar to some other single indicators, it has several shortcomings when considered separately. It is often influenced by irrational economic behavior, speculative policies and emotional feelings, all of them being more acute when concerning foreign agents (investors). The analyses of stock exchange data show, however, that there is enough rationale in stock exchange behavior to be considered as a meaningful domain of development. Poland can again serve as a good example. The Polish GDP never declined during the 2007–2013 crisis, however the stock exchange suffered a very substantial decline, exceeding 60% in the worst times. That was related

to a substantial decline in the profitability of Polish companies. Thus, the stock exchange index is a meaningful economic indicator supplementing other ones and contributing to the comprehensive picture of the economy despite its shortcomings when used separately from the others.
(Source of data: https://www.investing.com/indices/. For Luxembourg: https://markets.businessinsider.com/index/historical-prices/luxx)

3.2 Internal Economic Conditions

The internal functioning of the economy is characterized by the most popular economic indicators commonly used in analyses of the economic cycles. They are supplemented by some other indicators considered important.

GDP per capita does not require justification as an important element of socio-economic development. It is the most commonly used indicator of economic growth of the nation. By many – if not most – economists it is used as a single or as the most important indicator of economic development despite the fact that it concentrates on the production of goods and services. As such, it is often interpreted as "input" to more broadly understood socio-economic development.
(GDP per capita in USD, constant prices, 2010 PPP. *Source of data: World Bank*)

The production of electricity is an element of GDP, but we have decide to use it as an additional economic indicator of the nation's economic condition despite that this may be disputed from the purist statistical viewpoint. The production of electricity may sometimes even be used for the verification of GDP data. However, the discrepancies between the two of them may provide significant information on the domestic economic condition. For example, the production of electricity disproportionally lower than GDP constitutes a threat to a country's energy security and may hamper further economic growth.
(Source of data: OECD)

The share of accumulation in GDP is an indicator of GDP distribution, but it may be uncorrelated with GDP value. A relatively low share of accumulation in satisfactory GDP, especially during rapid GDP growth, may have a negative consequence for further development. Thus, it may be treated as a kind of "leading" indicator.
(Source of data: World Bank)

Yearly inflation is another indicator chosen according to Keynes' idea of seeking the models relevant for the contemporary world. It is important for socio-economic development because of its relation to GDP. Low inflation in a time of substantial GDP growth enlarges the socio-economic value of this growth, while high inflation has an opposite effect.
(Source of data: World Bank)

Households' final consumption per capita is another socio-economic indicator important for developmental processes. Contrary to GDP or other production and supply (input) variables, it may be interpreted as output from the well-being point of view. However, we have included it into economic rather than social variables because of its importance for economic growth. Insufficient growth of a household's consumption results in the decline of work motivation and so is detrimental to further development. On the other hand, an accelerated increase of individual consumption, together with social consumption, may hamper further development. (Data in USD, constant prices 2010. *Data source: World Bank*)

The unemployment rate is a second indicator which can be interpreted both from the social (well-being) and economic (employment, productive activity) point of view. We have included it into economic indicators because of its relation to GDP. Economic growth measured by GDP is usually related to a reduction in unemployment. However, that should be a quite substantial growth, e.g. above 3% (Okun 1962) Moreover, the direction of causality is sometimes opposite, since further development may be caused by higher employment caused by various political and business concerns. Since correlations between economic growth and unemployment may be quite non-canonical, unemployment is a significant addition to other economic variables.
(Inverted indicator. *Source of data: World Bank*)

The share of public debt in GDP is also characterized by a very ambiguous correlation with GDP and placing it in the composition of BDI indicators significantly enriches this indicator. It also neutralizes the big disputes in contemporary macroeconomics and economic policy regarding the extent to which the high share of debt limits growth. There is no doubt, however, that the benefits of a low share of debt in GDP can be huge, as well as limitations of development due to a large share of debt, and not only because of the low or high cost of debt service. Therefore, this fact should be reflected in indicators of stability and controllability of the socio-economic system, even if it is a significant "roughness" of GDP growth.
(Inverted indicator. *Source of data: OECD*)

The yearly increase in real average wages is another important economic indicator, which may change differently than GDP and which may have both economic and social connotations. From the economic point of view, it shows how well economic effectivity is remunerated. This presently constitutes a subject of vivid economic discussions and refined statistical analyses. Thus, we have included these "hard" objective indicators in the economic domain, leaving "soft" evaluations and expectations in their respective social domains.
(Source of data: OECD)

Business perception of the of the current activity tendency and production tendency in manufacturing, construction, retail trade and service. In the internal composition of the economic domain of the BDI index, we also use microeconomic business responses to survey questions regarding changes in their production,

orders, capacity utilization, employment intentions, etc. in production, construction, trade and services. This type of research has been conducted for a long time in order to improve GDP's informativeness. They are supposed to reveal GDP weaknesses associated, for example, with the specificity of its counting, artificial inflating and understating by its methodology of counting and the operation of governments, even a kind of creative accounting. They are also partly complemented by the informativeness of GDP-based public statistics. These indicators go in the same direction as our BDI indicator design, although as shown in the entire range of indicators that make up the BDI, this is just a small step in this direction. Taking as many as four such indices into account, separately for: manufacturing, construction, retail trade and service, it also allows to bring structural problems of economic changes which bypasses GDP.
(Source of data: OECD)

3.3 Current Social Conditions

The long history of attempts to replace or complement the GDP with a more comprehensive measure of social and economic development could be a topic for a separate book. Suffice it to say that the first phase of this work consisted of creating indices comprised of many social and demographic indicators (McGranahan et al. 1970). In brief, the idea was (and still is) to measure how "healthy, wealthy and wise" a society is, to use an old English adage. However, one may be materially well off, healthy, educated and highly qualified, and yet be unhappy. The conviction that good living conditions should be linked to a subjective feeling of well-being prompted by the emergence of a new field of science on the borders of economy, sociology and psychology (Diener and Seligman 2004; Frey 2008; Dutt and Radcliff 2009; Clark and Senik 2014; Brulé and Suter 2019, to mention only a few). The "economy of happiness", as it has come to be called, started to develop as a result of a long-lasting vivid debate concerning the question: "Does economic growth improve the human lot?" (Easterlin 1974; Clark and Senik 2011; Zagórski et al. 2014). The economy of happiness is paying attention to people's subjective feelings, especially their level of satisfaction. We adhere to the opinion that *"Measures of subjective well-being provide key information about people's quality of life... Quantitative measures of these subjective aspects hold the promise of delivering not just a good measure of quality of life per se, but also a better understanding of its determinants, reaching beyond people's income and material conditions"* (Stiglitz et al. 2010: 93). With this in mind, we describe social conditions with a series of both objective and subjective social indicators. We did not ask about satisfaction with life in general or a feeling of happiness, but about a subjective evaluation of different aspects of the social and economic situation that could be interpreted in terms of satisfaction. The World Happiness Index provides the most general measure of happiness in different countries (Helliwell et al. 2018). We would prefer to consider level of the society on this index as a correlate or even as an ultimate outcome of the obtained value of Balanced Development Index rather than as one of its components. While selecting social indicators, we took into account the goals set by the UN agenda "Transforming Our World: the 2030 Agenda for Sustainable Development" grossly influenced by Stiglitz, Sen and Fitousi ideas. The agenda identified 169 detailed targets which can be aggregated into 17 goals, such as: no poverty, no hunger, good health and well-being, quality education, gender equality, clean water and sanitation, affordable and clean energy, decent work and economic growth, industry innovation and infrastructure, reduced inequalities, responsible consumption and production, climate protection, life below water, life on land, peace, justice and strong institutions and partnership (Kanbur et al. 2018: 35–36). The final selection of social indicators is a compromise between the full list of important social concerns, perhaps even longer than that above, and the availability of reliable data.

Coefficients of birth and marriages as well as percentage of the population aged 0–14 constitute indicators of chances to maintain the proper structure and development of the population. Since all European societies experience such a negative demographic process as rising disproportion between youth and elderly, these indicators allow that situation to be assesd and are important for population policy.
(Sources of data: coefficient of births: Eurostat coefficient of marriages: OECD, population aged 0–14, % of the total: World Bank)

Infant mortality can be seen from the viewpoint of structural demographic processes, as above, and from the viewpoint of a healthy life.
(Per 1000 births, inverted index. *Source of data: World Bank*)

Public expenses for health service is an "input" indicator for such output as a healthy life.
(% GDP. *Source of data: OECD*)

Public welfare expenditure is commonly interpreted as indicating the governmental care for the welfare of citizens, similar to health service expenditure. However, it is more general and may have quite a different interpretation. While it is true that it indicates the care for the well-being of its citizens, we have found that welfare spending tends to rise in situations of deteriorating living conditions. Therefore, social welfare expenses are, in OECD European countries at least, more an indicator of crisis and a deterioration than the development.
(% GDP, inverted index. *Source of data: OECD*)

GINI coefficient of income inequality is a commonly used indicator of the vertical inequality. One of the criticisms of traditionally used development measures, GDP in particular, stresses that they don't take the socially important issue of distribution into consideration. The rapid growth of production, services and cumulation of wealth in the situation when a few rich people doing very well and many poor doing poorly can't be considered a characteristic of a well performing economy. For

example, the US economy seemed to be doing reasonably well when GDP was used as an indicator, but measures taking the distribution into account provided a markedly different picture (Stiglitz et al. 2018a, b: 62). The rising prominence of inequality and growing conscientiousness of its social consequences resulted in including its reduction into a list of UN Sustainable Development Goals and, in consequence, in many national social policies (Lustig 2018). Thus, we have included a GINI coefficient among current social indicators as characterizing vertical inequality in a more obvious way than the threat of poverty, which should also be interpreted in inequality terms.
(Inverted index. Source of data: OECD)

Consumption of energy from renewable sources and CO_2 emission are two different indicators related to such UN goals as clean energy and good climate, both important for sustainable development and good health.
(Sources of data: World Bank, Knoema, EDGAR)

The threat of poverty is a good indicator of material well-being. Since reliable and internationally comparable income data is not available, the number of households which are poor or threatened by poverty, usually obtained by means of special research, is a good income substitution, meaningful by itself. This indicator was previously called a "relative poverty". It shows how many households live on income below 60% of the average income. As such, it concerns the material level of living relative to other people and should hence be interpreted both in terms of material conditions and in terms of inequality.
(% of households, inverted index; *Source of data: Eurostat*)

Internet access can be interpreted as an indicator of social inclusion, especially the availability of information as well as communication with other people.
(% of households. *Source of data: Eurostat*)

Research and development employees indicate a nation's innovativeness and may also be interpreted as an outcome of good education and science.
(Per one million of the population. *Source of data: Eurostat*)

Youth unemployment rate is, in our opinion, a much better indicator of the labor market than general unemployment, since it may be considered as more socially harmful.
(Inverted indicator. *Source of data: World Bank*)

Robberies and homicides are two forms of social pathology which we have included as BDI components. Social pathology is seldom included by well-being and socio-economic development researchers in their indices, but good development should obviously not instigate pathological behavior.
(Both indicators per 100,000 population, inverted indicators. *Source of data: Knoema and Eurostat*)

Confidence in the government constitutes an element of broadly understood social trust. It reflects trust in those in the government as well as in governmental policies and governmental institutions. Trust matters for both political and economic

behavior, the latter being important for economic growth. It is related to GDP and also to such aspects of human conditions as: income, life satisfaction and even life expectancy. Countries of a high level of confidence in the government are also characterized by a higher level of objective indicators of bureaucratic efficiency, foreign direct investment, and even people's willingness to pay taxes. A good short overview of various research concerning these relations, all of them relevant for socio-economic development, is given by Algan (2018). Trust in the government can also be interpreted in terms of satisfaction with current politics, its actors and institutions, i.e. as an element of satisfaction with general, not only economic, living conditions.
(Source of data: Eurobarometer)

Subjective evaluations of (satisfaction with) a country's economic situation, a household's material situation and the labor market are subjective indicators collected similar to confidence in the government by sociological surveys. They constitute peoples' satisfaction with domains of socio-economic conditions most closely related to development. Satisfaction with material conditions of one's own household concerns directly the individual members of this household. Satisfaction with labor market concerns the individual less directly, especially if they have a stable job irrespective of more general labor market conditions. However, it is still very significant for them, especially if they or their family members experience unstable employment or are seeking job. Thus, together with material satisfaction, perceptions of labor market are not neutral to general life satisfaction. Satisfaction with government is usually not treated in literature and empirical research as a component of life satisfaction despite that political dissatisfaction grossly influence other feelings and social behavior of individuals. We have decided to consider in our work the satisfaction with these three different domains rather than with life in general. Since there is no good, internationally comparable data on household income, subjective evaluation of material living conditions of one's own household may be treated both as an element of life satisfaction and as a proxy for a real material situation, relative to other households in a country at least.
(Source of data: Eurobarometer)

3.4 Social Expectations

Ever since Hirschman's widely known metaphor of the "tunnel effect", supported by evidence from different countries, there has been general agreement that public expectations for future conditions often have a stronger effect on economic and political behavior, as well as on attitudes, than the actual situation and its evaluation (Hirschman 1981; Offe and Adler 1991; Zagórski 1994; Ravallion and Lokshin 2000; Buscha 2012; Cojocaru 2014; Krafft et al. 2018). This is consistent with the conviction that the consumer sentiment index, which includes consumers' economic expectations, is a leading rather than lagging indicator of economic changes (The University of Michigan 2018) and that it should be included in the Leading Economic Index – LEI (The Conference Board 2018). Moreover, the subjective perception of personal prospects for the future is, in Poland at least, a second important determinant of general life satisfaction, before such other determinants as: satisfaction with family, health, material living conditions, job etc. and right after satisfaction with friends and acquaintances (Koralewicz and Zagórski 2009). Thus, we have decided to construct an index of social expectations concerning both private and public domains.

Public expectations concerning the future economic situation of a country, a household's material condition and situation on the labor market as well as personal job are parallel to evaluations of current conditions in this respect included in a former group of indicators. **Expectations of better or worse future life in general** are an important addition concerning subjective well-being (happiness).
(Source of data: Eurobarometer)

Business expectations in manufacturing and retail trade are included among social rather than economic indicators, since – contrary to business perception of current activity – they are not based on hard economic data on one's own business but on subjective feelings associated with expectations in other domains of social and economic life.
(Source of data: OECD)

Both public evaluations of various domains of social conditions and expectations of the future conditions are subjective measures of well-being. *"Measures of subjective well-being provide key information about people's quality of life... Quantitative measures of these subjective aspects hold the promise of delivering not just a good measure of quality of life per se, but also a better understanding of its determinants, reaching beyond people's income and material conditions"* (Stiglitz et al. 2010: 93).

Each of these simple indicators was standardized. The indicators of bad conditions were inverted (multiplied by −1). Four middle-level indices were calculated as an arithmetic means of standardized variables belonging to the index. The BDI was then calculated as an arithmetic mean of middle-level indices).

The BDI measures not only a broad spectrum of socioeconomic well-being, but also the level of balance of the system as a whole. Imbalance is reflected by the excessive value of standard deviations of the four BDI composite components. However, we do not *apriori* define any specific value of standard deviation which would specify the borderline between balance and imbalance. Instead, we are interested in examining the influence exerted by standard deviation on trends of socioeconomic change measured by the BDI.

The composite index is a measure not only of good socioeconomic conditions, but we hope that it also indicates a system's controllability, understood as its susceptibility to stimuli coming from the reforming policies of the center. When the BDI is high and growing, the chances are that reforms will be accepted. This is the "window of opportunity" which closes when the index starts to fall and when reforms become increasingly needed in order to stop further decline. In case of inconsistency between subjective and objective indicators, one should consider the reasons

behind the negative social mood and seek to improve a system considered by numerous groups as unjust and uncertain instead of concentrating on "hard" economic results.
(Source of data: Eurobarometer)

4 To Weight or not to Weight?

As discussed above, two economic and two social domains of development are distinguished in our research. Each of them is measured by a middle-level composite index constructed of several detailed indicators of equal weight. The four middle-level indices are then compressed into a general Balanced Development Index, also with equal weights.

In order to measure *balanced development*, one has to use a *balanced index*, i.e. index comprising both social and economic indicators, each given the same importance. Particular detailed indicators and middle level indices contributing to the BDI are not weighed in our approach (practically one can say that they are equally weighted by 1), because of the assumption of their equal importance, an approach already suggested by Saisana and Tarantola (2002). There is no theoretical ground to say which indicators are more important than others.

Neither detailed indicators, nor middle-level indices are weighed for methodological reasons as well, since there are no generally accepted rules, either theoretical or methodological, for weighing indicators aggregated into composite indices (Ebert and Welsch 2004).

There are two most frequently used ways of weighing various domains of development and their indicators: expert opinions, sometimes replaced by public opinion, and statistical methods, predominantly various kinds of factor analysis. Expert wisdom is not applied here as being much too subjective. Adding one or two experts to an expert panel may dramatically change the results. Public opinion, when used instead of an expert opinion, may give different weights to different developmental domains in different rapidly changing circumstances. Moreover, the weights given by experts or public opinion to different domains of development may substantially differ between different countries. On the other hand, such statistical methods as various kinds of factor analysis are based on correlation or covariance matrices. This is a serious issue as our analysis concerns just 16 years of socioeconomic development in only 22 countries. In such a small sample, updating the data by adding 1 or 2 years or adding one or two countries may change the correlations and, in consequence, the statistically determined weights, putting attempts to create a universal and stable system of weighting into question. Moreover, rigorously applied statistical rules should exclude highly correlated indicators from the factor analysis, since this method is very sensitive to collinearity and produces very unstable results in such circumstances. Most indicators used in developmental studies, our study included, are highly correlated, so the problem of collinearity would be paramount. All in all, we have decided not to apply different weights for both substantive and methodological reasons.

5 Development and Socio-economic Balance

As it was already said, the BDI is geared not only to measure level of socio-economic development of contemporary societies. We believe that it can indicate the controllability of socio-economic systems or, in other words, the ability to properly perform governance functions and to initiate and implement development programs. Such programs (reforms) enable the survival and development of systems in turbulent environments, as examples of countries included in this study clearly demonstrate.

The concept of functional balance is of fundamental importance for the BDI. It was originally developed in the studies of organizational dynamics for companies (Kaplan and Norton 1996), organizations (March 1981) and larger more complex systems (Weintraub 1974). Norton and Kaplan used four dimensions of functional balance dynamic of the firm: finance, clients, internal processes and development. The BDI uses four macro perspectives (external and internal economic performance, social expectations and current social situation) to assess the dynamics of socio-economic systems. This is a unique mix of social and economic factors.

Our concept of a system's balance preconditioning socio-economic development is based on several complementary theoretical presumptions, partially confirmed by our study of 22 countries:

1. The idea of balanced development implies equal importance of its social and economic aspects. This may be apparent in the case of misguided economic growth, which does not bring an improvement in the quality of life of a majority of the population despite the growing supply of some unneeded material product and misguided services. On the other hand, while comparative analyses suggest that progress, broadly understood, can be achieved without excessive reliance on level of production and income (Natoli and Zuhair 2011), the question remains whether such an achievement can be long standing and generally approved. Economic growth and improvements in social life conditions need to go hand in hand. There is no reason to assume the superiority of one over the other (for a discussion see Sirgy 2011).
2. Our concept of balance (equilibrium) rests upon the assumption that a certain degree of balance is needed to control the system and assure its survival in a turbulent environment, while a certain level of imbalance is needed to instigate development. This is consistent with Pareto's concept of functional equilibrium (Pareto 1963; Powers 2012). Imbalances occur when individual elements (four BDI middle level indices) excessively diverge from one another over time. This idea is rooted in the work of Lyapunov, a nineteenth century Russian mathematician considered one of the pioneers of systems theory (Lyapunov 1992). Thus, disruption of the systems balance is reflected in an excessive increase of standard deviations between BDI components.
3. Our hypothesis is that a prolonged static equilibrium, i.e. a persistent high degree of congruence between BDI components, leads to a lack of growth (stagnation), to "sticking points" in Pareto's sense (Powers 2012) and sometimes even to

decline. This hypothesis was confirmed by the dynamic analysis of the BDI in Poland (Kozminski et al. 2016) The so-called "dynamic equilibrium", i.e. parallel growth of all components of the index without changing proportions between them, may have a similar hampering effect on further development. However, N. Tuma and M. T. Hannan (1984) have stressed that social systems seldom achieve and maintain a dynamic equilibrium.

4. We assume that imbalance may pull the general index of development both up and down. Putting it simply, it can have both positive and negative effects. When excessive imbalance prevails over a long period of time, it threatens the controllability of the system, its responsiveness to managerial and governance impulses and hampers or stops its further development, as prolonged static equilibrium also does. However, some imbalance is needed to knock the system out of stagnation.
5. We do not hypothesize about the optimum level and persistence of imbalance, but simply include the measure of balance into our analytical model in order to find out when the development trend stops or changes, and in the case of the latter, in which direction. We are interested in the level of balance of four domains of development embraced by the BDI. The standard deviation between four middle level indices (components of BDI) is used as a measure of balance. A similar kind of approach was taken in the US in the 1970s as a consequence of the L.A. riots of 1968. The dynamic macro-social indicator model, taking into the account imbalance between various aspects of the situation, was used by police authorities to predict a sudden increase in crime rates and riots. Such a model enabled law enforcement authorities to take available counter-measures and to allocate police resources adequately (Land and Felson 1976).

A review of balance between four composite elements of the BDI measured by the standard deviation between them, shows that balance is an important condition of change and reform. Our presupposition was that it may be either detrimental (dysfunctional) or beneficial for the socio-economic system, depending on the degree of imbalance.

Our analysis allows us a well justified hypothesis that, similar to the cognitive dissonance theory (Festinger 1962) the optimal level of imbalance (dissonance, incongruence) between the four aspects of socio-economic development instigate the change, whereas the absence of any dissonance leads to stagnation. This is consistent with the commonsense "development through crises". Figure 1.4 based on data for all European OECD countries in 16 years, presents the dependence of the BDI level in a given year on the standard deviation of four BDI components a year earlier.

It is evident from the Fig. 1.4 that the larger the imbalance (higher standard deviation) between four BDI components in a given year, the higher the BDI in a following year, but to a certain point. The dependence is curvilinear in nature. The level of a country's socio-economic development in a given year is extremely low in the condition of full balance (congruence) between four middle-level components of the BDI (standard deviation <1) and in the condition of very high imbalance between them (standard deviation >4). It is highest when the imbalance is moderate

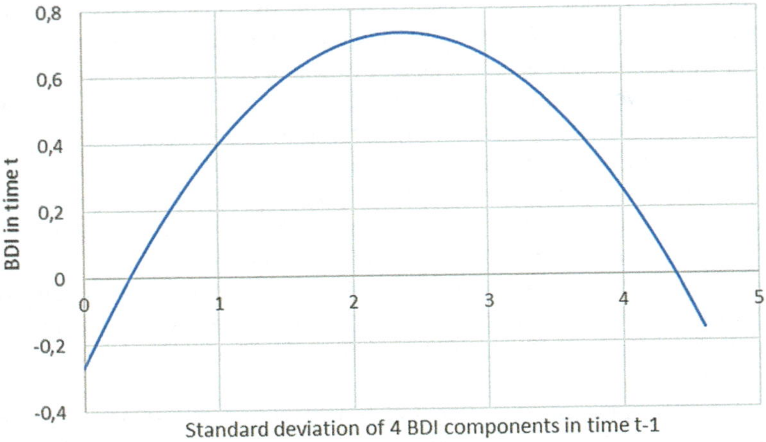

Fig. 1.4 Standard deviation between the four BDI components and the value of the BDI in the following years (estimation based on o.l.s. regression). Note: O.l.s. regression estimated for 396 cases (22 countries × 18 years)

(between 2 and 3). The BDI value rises fast with growing imbalance until the standard deviation approaches 2 and slows down after that point. When the standard deviation exceeds 3, the BDI value declines very quickly. Of course, there are no cases of standard deviation equal zero or higher than 4 in our data, but we have decided to present a full theoretical curve to show potentially possible extremes. However, our analysis clearly shows that the low developed European countries are characterized either by a very low or by very high dissonance between the BDI components i.e. between four realms of development. A moderate imbalance (dissonance) is a feature of highly developed countries. Thus, it can be concluded that a moderate imbalance is the best condition for socio-economic development.

Chapter 2
International Comparative Analysis of BDI Dynamics

1 International Differences in the Level of Socioeconomic Development

European OECD countries differ to a large degree in terms of their socioeconomic development as measured by the BDI. The most general measure of development is the mean for all the years under analysis, calculated for each country. A comparison of these mean values will, for now, eliminate the fluctuations caused by the last financial crisis and other changes in economic and social conditions (Fig. 2.1).

Sweden, Denmark, Luxembourg, Ireland, Finland and the Netherlands are clearly in the forefront. These are the countries that are not only rich, but also implementing extensive welfare state policies. Great Britain and Austria are still above 22 countries average. Estonia, France and Czech Republic are close to average BDI value. Countries in the third group, Slovenia, Germany and Belgium are not much below the average and they differ slightly between each other. Noticeably below the average BDI are such countries as Slovak Republic, Spain, Latvia and Italy. There is a visible gap between them and the group of the least developed countries, namely: Portugal, Poland, Greece and Hungary.

Clearly, the ranking of countries by the mean BDI for 19 years is not quite in accordance with the stereotypes based on gross national income, divisions into the north and south or a post-communist status. It is evident, however, that countries with a high level of economic development combined with a welfare state policy are at the forefront.

A. K. Koźmiński et al., *The Balanced Development Index for Europe's OECD Countries, 1999–2017*, SpringerBriefs in Economics,
https://doi.org/10.1007/978-3-030-39240-6_2

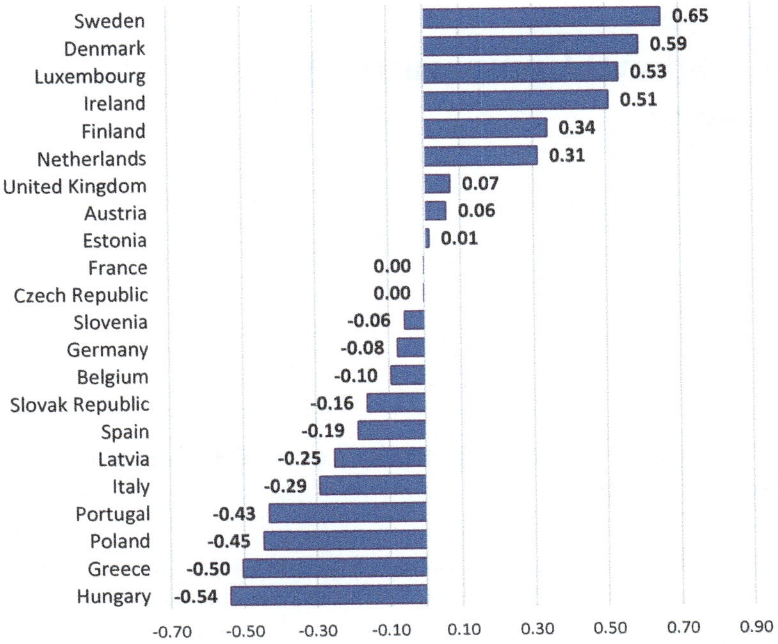

Fig. 2.1 Mean BDI for 22 countries, 1999–2017

2 BDI and Other Indices

The first question prior to further analyses is why should the BDI index be used instead of GDP or in addition to it? In other words, how does the BDI differ from GDP and what are its strengths? These two indicators should be compared for different countries and periods in order to answer such questions. Table 2.1 presents a comparative ranking of 22 countries in terms of their BDI and GDP in three different years:

- 1999, a year characterized by an exceptionally good economic situation in Europe,
- 2009, the worst year of the last economic crisis in Europe,
- 2015, the year considered as the definitive end of the crisis and the beginning of a new phase of growth.

Table 2.1 justifies the following statements:

1. Generally speaking, in all periods (before, during and after the crisis) the higher the BDI, the higher the GDP. This is not surprising, since GDP is one of many BDI components. However, there are several significant exceptions from this rule.

Table 2.1 Ranking of 22 countries using the BDI and GDP indices for the years 1999, 2009 and 2015

Ranking								
1999			2009			2015		
Country	BDI	GDP	Country	BDI	GDP	Country	BDI	GDP
Ireland	**1**	**5**	Luxembourg	1	1	**Ireland**	**1**	**2**
Sweden	**2**	**8**	**Sweden**	**2**	**6**	**Denmark**	**2**	**4**
Luxembourg	3	1	**Denmark**	**3**	**4**	**Sweden**	**3**	**5**
Finland	**4**	**11**	Ireland	4	3	Luxembourg	4	1
Netherlands	5	3	**Finland**	**5**	**9**	Netherlands	5	3
Denmark	6	2	Netherlands	6	2	**United Kingdom**	**6**	**9**
Spain	**7**	**13**	Austria	7	5	**Finland**	**7**	**10**
France	**8**	**10**	**Czech Republic**	**8**	**16**	**Czech Republic**	**8**	**14**
United Kingdom	**9**	**12**	**Slovenia**	**9**	**15**	**Estonia**	**9**	**18**
Portugal	**10**	**14**	France	10	10	Germany	10	7
Greece	**11**	**15**	Belgium	11	7	Austria	11	6
Austria	12	4	Germany	12	8	**Latvia**	**12**	**22**
Belgium	13	6	**Slovak Republic**	**13**	**18**	Spain	13	13
Germany	14	7	United Kingdom	14	11	**Slovak Republic**	**14**	**16**
Slovenia	**15**	**16**	Spain	15	13	France	15	11
Italy	16	9	Greece	16	14	Slovenia	16	15
Czech Republic	17	17	Italy	17	12	Belgium	17	8
Latvia	**18**	**22**	Portugal	18	17	**Poland**	**18**	**19**
Slovak Republic	19	19	**Estonia**	**19**	**20**	Italy	19	12
Estonia	20	20	**Poland**	**20**	**21**	Hungary	20	20
Hungary	21	18	Hungary	21	19	Portugal	21	17
Poland	22	21	Latvia	22	22	Greece	22	21

Note: In bold are the countries higher in ranking by BDI than by GDP

2. There are five countries in the forefront, occupying the highest position according to both BDI and GDP. These are Ireland, Sweden, Luxembourg, the Netherlands and Denmark. In 1999, Finland was also in this group, but the impact of the crisis was so heavy on this country that it found itself nowadays definitely below the level of the other five.
3. The positions of the most developed countries in ranking by BDI differed from their position in ranking by GDP more before the crisis than during it and after it. The crisis appears to have made the two hierarchies more similar. Denmark and Sweden, two Scandinavian states with a strong welfare state tradition, are now slightly higher in the BDI compared to GDP.
4. The next group of countries was characterized by a relative high level of general socioeconomic development in 1999, incommensurately higher than the GDP. The crisis resulted in a drop in their relative positions in BDI ranking to positions much more similar to those occupied in terms of GDP. These are Spain,

France and Portugal, the countries believed to suffer from the crisis the most. Greece has to be added to this group. One can assume that the relatively high socioeconomic level of these countries prior to the crisis resulted largely from a welfare state policy incommensurate with the size of the gross national income and economic potential however measured. Such a situation became impossible in time of the crisis, leading to political complications and austerity measures. This shows the usefulness of the BDI as a more universal index than the GDP.

5. The post-communist countries present an interesting case. Before the crisis they were low in both BDI and GDP rankings. While the crisis lowered the relative position of a considerable number of countries from western and southern Europe in terms of the general socioeconomic situation, the post-communist countries improved their relative (which does not always mean absolute) position in this respect. This refers to the Czech Republic, Slovakia, Latvia, Poland and Estonia (not so much to Slovenia and Hungary). It would appear that the societies in these countries experienced faith and satisfaction caused by the system transformation, believing in a "bright future" (including personal and business optimism). Such feelings reinforced by real living conditions improving till 1999 for majority of population, made these societies psychologically better prepared for the effects of the crisis, thus influencing a higher BDI value.
6. The crisis led to a greater congruency between ranking of countries in terms of the general socioeconomic situation and the gross domestic products. That has happened primarily due to relative lowering of socioeconomic level in countries where it had been higher than the GDP ("average" and less developed western and southwestern countries). There was, however, a relative improvement of the general socioeconomic situation in post-communist countries in the same time. The end of the crisis was characterized by a more or less similar improvement of general socioeconomic conditions and GDP without a return to the pre-crisis disproportions, which may have possibly been one of the reason of the crisis in the first place.

There are several widely used indices developed in a paradigm of "beyond GDP" or "social well-being (SWB)". The basic question is whether they describe somewhat different realms of socio-economic conditions or whether they constitute the indicators of the same or almost the same general concept. Designing and implementing a new index would not make much sense, if it measures the same phenomenon in the same way as those previously applied. Thus, BDI should be compared to at least some indices that have been earlier developed and used. Similar to comparing GDP with other indices, the BDI will be compared to Better Life Index (OECD 2018), Human Development Index (UNDP 2018) and World Happiness Index (WHR 2019). For the sake of simplicity, we will use 2017 data only.

Different concepts behind compared indices and – in consequence – their different composition result in somewhat different ranking of European countries by these indices (Table 2.2).

Detailed differences in rankings look a bit chaotic and difficult to interpret. They depend on very particular configurations of simple indicators contributing to the

Table 2.2 Ranking of 22 European countries by different development indices, 2017

Balanced Development Index	Better Life Index	Human Development Index	World Happiness Index
1. Ireland	1. Denmark	1. Ireland	1. Finland
2 Denmark	2. Sweden	2. Germany	2. Denmark
3. Luxembourg	3. Finland	3. Sweden	3. Netherlands
4. Netherlands	4. Netherlands	4. Netherlands	4. Sweden
5. Sweden	5. Belgium	5. Denmark	5. Austria
6. Finland	6. Germany	6. United Kingdom	6. Ireland
7. Germany	7. Luxembourg	7. Finland	7. Germany
8. Czech Republic	8. Ireland	8. Belgium	8. Belgium
9. Estonia	9. United Kingdom	9. Austria	9. Luxembourg
10. Slovenia	10. Austria	10. Luxembourg	10. United Kingdom
11. Austria	11. France	11. France	11. Czech Republic
12. France	12. Spain	12. Slovenia	12. France
13. Slovakia	13. Slovenia	13. Spain	13. Spain
14. United Kingdom	14. Czech Republic	14. Czech Republic	14. Slovakia
15. Latvia	15. Estonia	15. Italy	15. Poland
16. Portugal	16. Italy	16. Estonia	16. Italy
17. Belgium	17. Slovakia	17. Greece	17. Slovenia
18. Hungary	18. Poland	18. Poland	18. Latvia
19. Poland	19. Portugal	19. Slovakia	19. Estonia
20. Spain	20. Latvia	20. Portugal	20. Hungary
21. Italy	21. Hungary	21. Latvia	21. Portugal
22. Greece	22. Greece	22. Hungary	22. Greece

different indices. However, the positions of countries on these indices don't seem to differ greatly. There is a clearly visible group of five countries of high ranks on all four indices, namely Denmark, Sweden, Finland, Ireland and The Netherlands. They may be characterized as economically developed welfare-states. There is also a distinct group of six countries with low values of all four indices. These are Greece, Hungary, Latvia, Italy, Poland and Portugal, i.e. less developed South-West as well as some "post-communist" countries.

Such simplified comparison can't tell very much about level of similarity or dissimilarity between ranking by the four indices. That should be determined by looking at correlation coefficients (Table 2.3).

Consistent with possible expectations, Table 2.3 shows quite high correlations between the BDI and other indices. Pearson's correlations of the BDI rank from .710 with the Human Development Index to .756 with GDP. However, these correlations are significantly lower than the almost perfect (approaching .90) correlations of GDP with other indices (see Table 1.2, p. 6).

Surprisingly, despite the inclusion of many economic indicators in the BDI and weighting its two composite economic middle level indices equally to two social

Table 2.3 Correlations between BDI and other social and economic rankings of 22 European countries, 2017

Selected indices	BDI
Pearson's correlation	
GDP	.756
Better Life Index	.737
Human Development Index	.710
World Happiness Index	.722

ones, the correlation between GDP and BDI is lower than those between GDP and the indices which do not pay much attention to the economy. Since BDI is more comprehensive and attaches equal weight to the social and economic aspect of human development, it differs from other compared indices more that they differ between themselves, despite some of them almost completely neglecting economic conditions. One can even pose a question, why replace or supplement the GDP by the Human Development Index, Better Life Index or World Happiness index if the results of their application are almost identical?

Our analyses suggest almost perfect interchangeability between GDP, the Better Life, Human Development and World Happiness indices, and greater specificity of the Balanced Development Index. BDI is evidently more comprehensive than other compared indices. Its usefulness should be proven by further analyses. The possibility to use the general BDI index and, additionally, its four composite social and economic components is especially important in this respect.

3 Changes of the BDI and the Four Domains of Socio-economic Development

One of the strengths of the BDI, as already mentioned, is the possibility of comparing trends in changes of the four composite components. We will compare changing means of their values for all 22 countries, i.e. for the whole OECD – EU.

The BDI shows the effects of the last financial crisis much more clearly than GDP. Though the directions and times of changes of both indices as well as four BDI components are similar, the BDI changes are much more radical than GDP changes. Out of all four domains of development, only current social conditions change almost the same way as GDP, while the changes in three remaining BDI domains are more pronounced (Figs. 2.2 and 2.3).

The socioeconomic situation of Europe, measured by the BDI, was characterized by a slight deterioration in the period from 2000 to 2003 despite a continuously growing GDP. That was mostly caused by a strong decline in social expectations and – to a lesser extent – by internal economic conditions, while actual social conditions remained at a level very similar to GDP.

From 2003 to 2007, shortly before the crisis, all countries featured a BDI growth more rapid than GDP growth. This lead to an exceptionally good situation in the

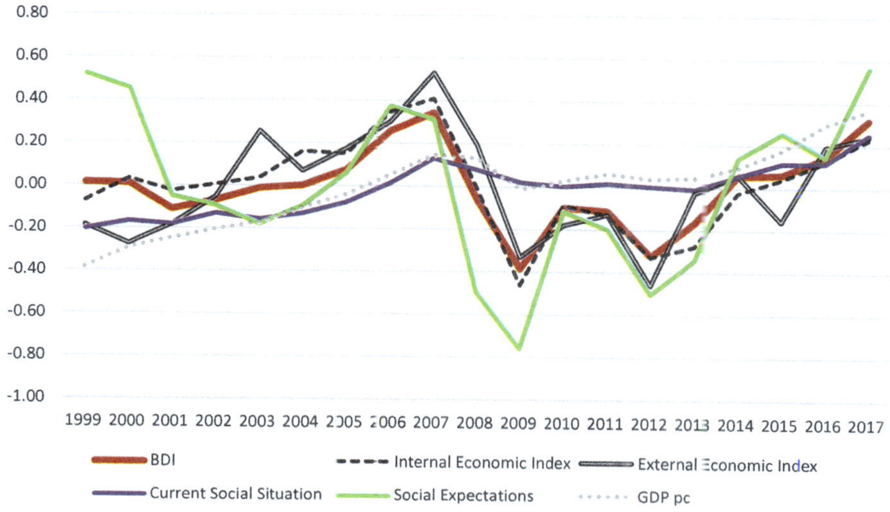

Fig. 2.2 The BDI index, its four components and GDP per capita, average for 22 European countries, 1999–2017

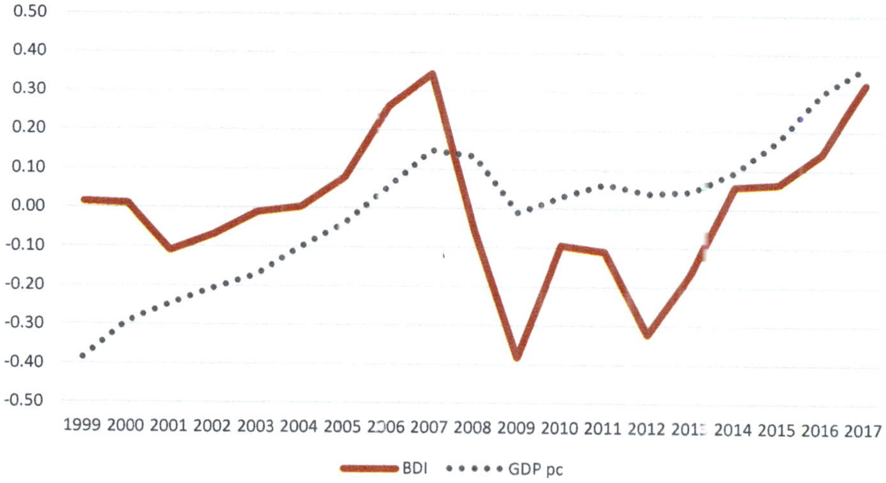

Fig. 2.3 Changes in the mean values of BDI and GDP in all 22 countries

pre-crisis 2007, the BDI index being relatively much higher than the GDP. Such a discrepancy resulted from the very good functioning of European countries' economies in their international context and – to a somewhat smaller extent – by the high level of peoples' optimism towards the future. The current social conditions did not improve and did not differ much from the GDP level, though they were slightly below it, while they were above it until 2003. In the period immediately before the crisis in 2007, the BDI was at record high level. It can be said that there was practically a feeling of euphoria in the European countries, which included a positive social mood and faith in a better future caused by good objective conditions. It is hard to resist the impression that it was a kind of "overheating" that "must have ended" in a crisis.

The global crisis first led to a violent deterioration of the overall socioeconomic situation measured by the BDI and then to a drop in GDP. The GDP started to decline a year later than the BDI and its drop was much less violent. Later changes of the BDI and GDP were congruent, but even so the general socioeconomic situation changed much more than the GDP. Moreover, while internal economic and social conditions and social expectations in the pre-crisis period were relatively better than the level the GDP suggested, they became relatively much worse during the crisis. Social expectations deteriorated the most. Despite a quicker improvement of the BDI in the post-crisis period, it is still relatively worse than the national product would suggest.

Social expectations were changing in the entire analyzed period much more than all other indices. That may indicate a tendency of peoples' overreaction to actual economic and social conditions.

It should be emphasized that the decline of the BDI index and all four its composite components, especially the external economic situation and social expectation, preceded the changes in GDP in 2007–2009, hence they can be considered as leading indicators. One should also note that the amplitude of changes of social expectations was much greater than the amplitude of changes of the other composite constituents of the DBI. This is proof of an overreaction of societies to the changing situation.

Despite the significant level of covariation of all four groups of indicators in all countries (Cronbach's alpha coefficient = .791), the most dramatic changes can be observed in the domain of social expectations. This would confirm the opinion about some kind of "hysteria" that seems to be "driven", to a large extent, by all kinds of media: official, political, commercial and social, as well as the emerging new paradigm of populist and emotional political leadership in many countries around the world.

Fluctuations and changes of the BDI are more frequent and more radical than changes in the economic situation measured by commonly used economic indicators, such as GDP. The socio-economic situation is more volatile and more "capricious" than the volume of sold goods and services.

All the results presented above lead us to the conclusion that the BDI describes the development of a country better than the GDP does. The index is much "richer" and more sensitive than the GDP.

For each of the analyzed countries, a more detailed analysis of the BDI cycles could be carried out. To make the comparisons easier, we have arbitrarily divided 22 countries into five groups: Those with a high, medium-high, medium, medium-low and low average BDI index (Figs. 2.4, 2.5, 2.6, 2.7, and 2.8).

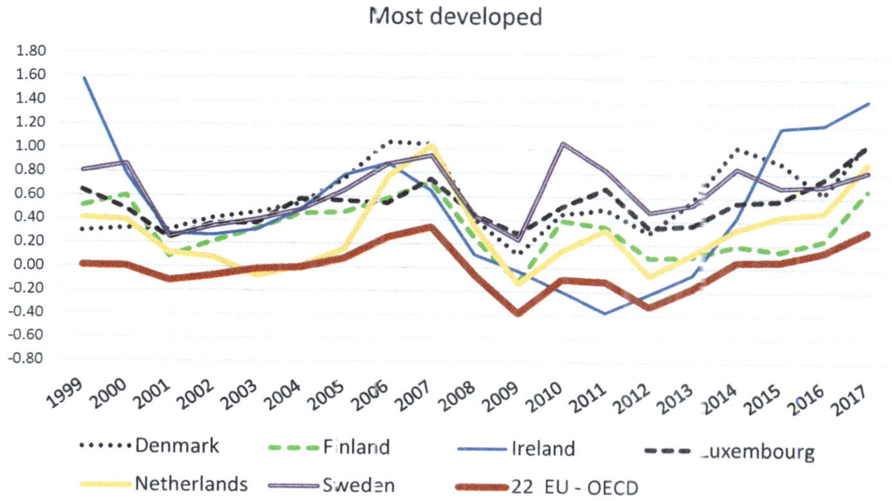

Fig. 2.4 Socio-economic development in most developed European countries, 1999–2017

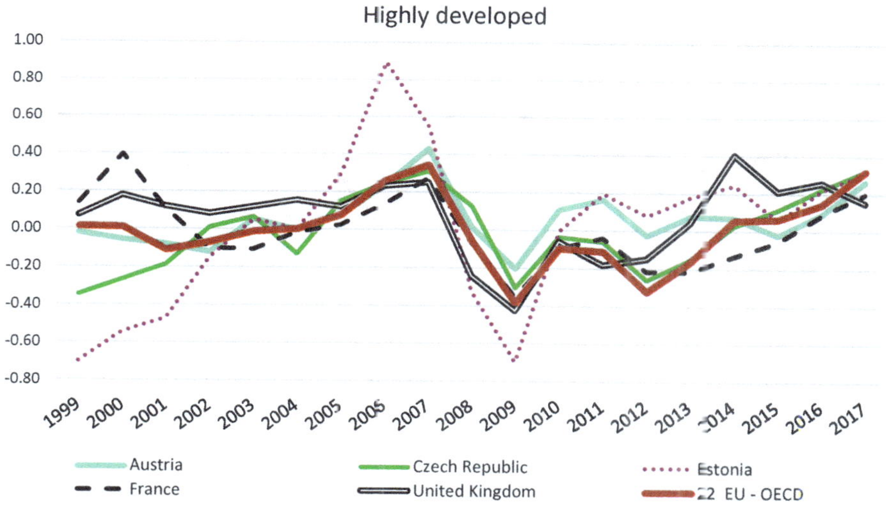

Fig. 2.5 Socio-economic development in highly developed European countries, 1999–2017

In practically all of the countries, the BDI index indicates a very good socioeconomic situation just before the most recent crisis and shows two evident crisis cycles. The first cycle resulted in an unfavorable situation in 2009, the second in 2012. There are several exceptions to this rule. Ireland was the only one of the highly developed countries to experience a single crisis cycle peaking in 2011–2012, after which exceptionally rapid recovery followed. The two Baltic states, Estonia

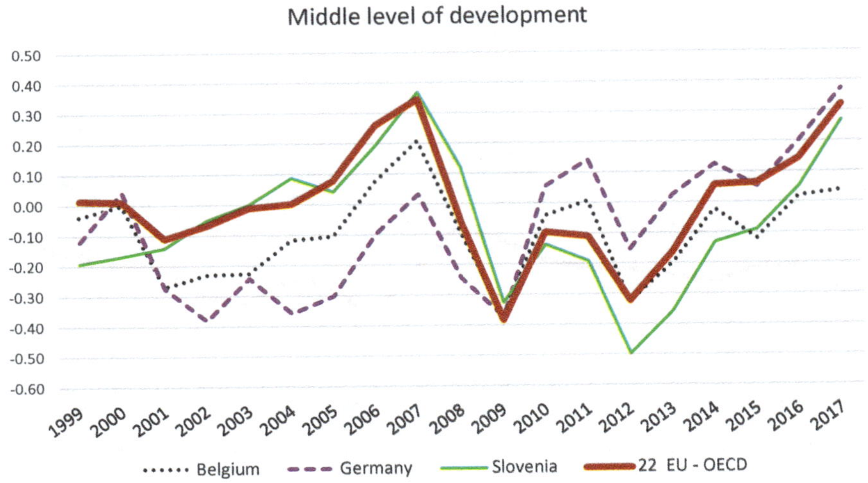

Fig. 2.6 Socio-economic development in middle level European countries, 1999–2017

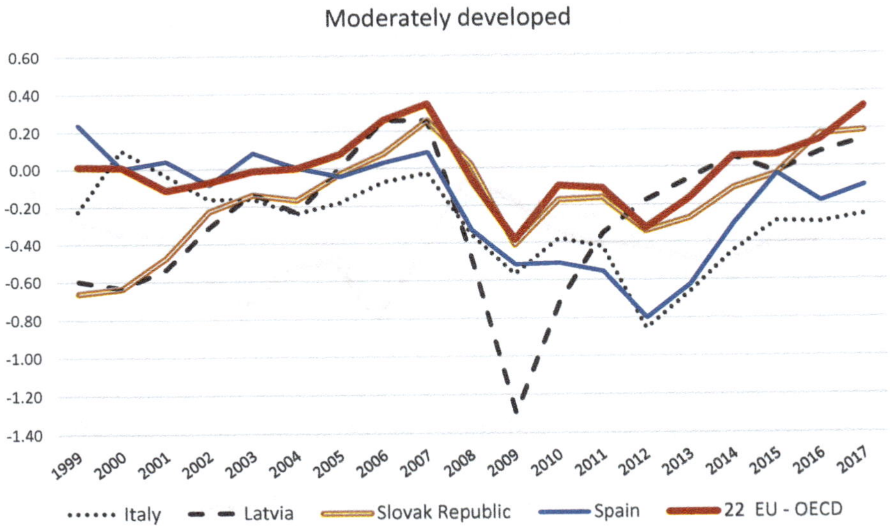

Fig. 2.7 Socio-economic development in moderately low developed European countries, 1999–2017

(in the "highly developed" group) and Latvia as well as Slovakia (in the "moderately developed group), started from a relatively low position at the beginning of the century, but their overcoming of the crisis led them to a level resembling that of the other countries in their group.

Regarding the group of low BDI, the changes in Greece took a very specific course. At the beginning of the century Greece was highest in the group, whereas in

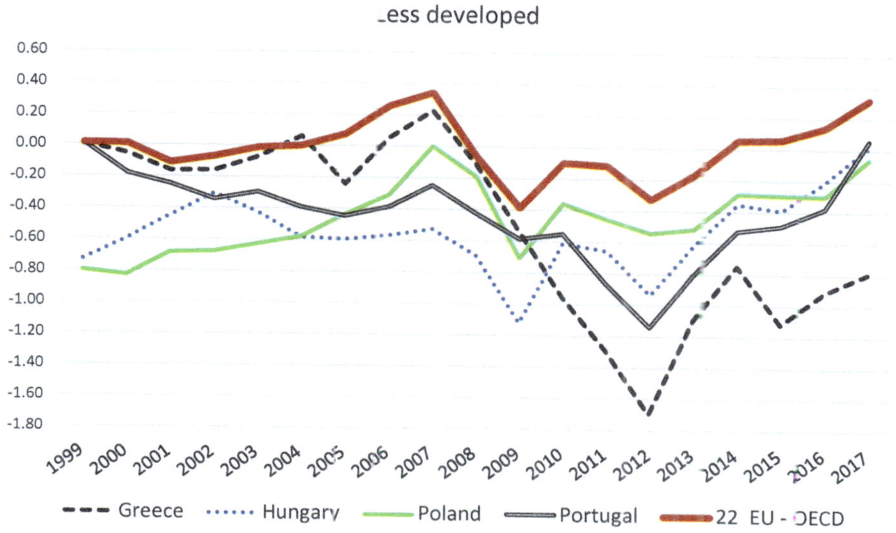

Fig. 2.8 Socio-economic development in less developed European countries, 1999–2017

2015 it was in last place in Europe. The case of Greece is so interesting that it will be developed further in this book.

The relatively small amplitude of BDI changes is a characteristic feature of countries near the European mean. The countries with both a high and a low level of socioeconomic development are more susceptible to crisis-related changes than the countries close to the mean.

4 Policy Windows: Four Types of Economies

Labeling countries as "frugal", "austere", "unreasonable", "reckless spenders" etc. is a common practice in the public debate. It applies, in particular, to distinctions between the "South" and "North" or "East" and "West" of Europe. Our research shows that there may be some truth to this. OECD countries included in our sample demonstrate highly divergent but relatively stable and durable attitudes in their choices of fiscal and monetary, commercial, industrial and social policies. Such attitudes are difficult but in the long run possible to change. They have political and by the same token emotional underpinnings.

One conceptual approach for understanding policy change is provided by the work of John W. Kingdon on "policy windows". Kingdon (1995) suggests that for putting an issue on the political agenda, three "streams" must be aligned: the problem stream (the subjective political assessment of a gap between actual and desirable situation), the policy stream (are there policy alternatives that can be implemented?), and the political stream (are politicians willing and able to make a policy change?). When these three streams converge, a window of opportunity is open and an action can be taken.

Our understanding of policy window is a change of policies aimed at improving the steerability and stability of the socio-economic system. Thanks to the four groups of BDI middle level indices, we are able to build a typology of countries. We analyze the correlations between our middle level indices: external economic (a year earlier) and internal economic, and between social expectations (a year earlier) and the internal economic situation. The first correlation shows how strongly countries are dependent on the external (international) economic situation. This is a serious policy challenge, because such dependence carries both opportunities (foreign direct investment, exports, debt financing etc.) and threats (unilateral profiteering by foreign entities). This challenge determines policy choices.

The second correlation between social expectations (a year before) and the economic situation (the following year) shows how *vox populi* precedes policies or – in other words – how emotional they are. In strictly economic terms the choice between more and less emotional policies spells out as preference of consumption over investment or vice versa. This is an eternal economic dilemma: to consume in emotional search of instant gratification or to invest in rational hope for bigger and more stable future rewards. This applies to societies organized in the form of democratic states as well as to individuals. This dilemma is associated with a great dispute in economic theory from J.M. Keynes to the present day on the subject of the rationality and the irrationality of the expectations of economic entities. The main explanation of the collapse of the demand driven Keynenesian policy in the mid-1970s after its 30 "golden years" was the indication that economic entities are becoming more and more rational and predict the negative consequences (such as inflation) of the state's discretionary and emotional economic policy. That was explained in the so-called "Lucas (1981) critique". We can explain the recent renaissance of Keynesian thought during the 2007–2013 economic crisis in a similar way. "We all became Keynesian" as O. Blanchard put it in 2010 quoting Richard Nixon's famous saying from 1971. Such a policy change confirms the hypothesis that expectations become more "emotional" and even "animal" during the crisis. They become further from rationality and realism (Akerlof and Shiller 2010). Therefore, the BDI index, including expectations, opens interesting opportunities for contributing to this eternal dispute of learned economists and politicians.

If the correlation between earlier external economic functioning and internal economic situation a year later exceeds .50, one can conclude that the external economic situation influences the internal one very strongly. That is apparent in such countries as: Greece, Ireland, Portugal, Italy, Poland, Spain and Slovakia. These are countries strongly dependent on exports, imports and inflows of capital from abroad. Downturns in the economic situation abroad carry a considerable risk of worsening the internal economic situation or even recession. In countries strongly dependent on economic external factors, the external situation of the previous year can serve as a good predictor of the current economic situation (Table 2.4).

Table 2.4 "Dependent" and "independent" economies, 22 European countries 1999–2017

Country	Pearson's correlations between earlier external economic situation (in year $t-1$) and current internal economic situation (in year t).
"Dependent" economies	**.644**
Greece	.811
Ireland	.810
Portugal	.656
Italy	.632
Poland	.582
Spain	.510
Slovakia	.506
"Independent" economies	**.238**
Estonia	.456
Slovenia	.455
Czech Republic	.402
Latvia	.400
France	.386
Luxembourg	.258
Hungary	.220
United Kingdom	.190
Austria	.172
Germany	.168
Denmark	.155
Netherlands	.117
Finland	.101
Sweden	.077
Belgium	.015

The key factor determining the future are social expectations regarding the socio-economic situation of individuals, their families and countries. The countries of low correlation between external economic functioning and the internal economic situation later on can be called "sovereign" countries. They are quite independent of the rest of the world. In Europe, they are conducting socio-economic policies in line with the society's expectations.

Conversely, in "fragile", generally less developed countries, strongly dependent upon external economic conditions, the current functioning of the economy is more dependent upon "hard" economic conditions imposed by external environments.

From the point of view of the dependence of the current economic situation upon the previous social expectations (measured by the Pearson's correlation coefficient), we can distinguish "emotional" economies. They are usually also characterized by a low share of investment and a high share of consumption in GDP. "Rational" economies are characterized by a much lower correlation between social expectations in the previous year and the current economic situation. They also feature a higher share of investments and a lower share of

Table 2.5 "Emotional" and "Rational" economies, 22 European countries 1999–2017

Country	Pearson's correlations between earlier social expectations (in year $t-1$) and current economic situation (in year t)	Investment share in GDP (in %)	Consumption share in GDP (in %)
"Emotional" economies	**.668**	**19**	**56**
Greece	.866	12	70
Portugal	.765	15	66
Czech Republic	.738	25	49
Spain	.726	20	58
United Kingdom	.722	17	65
Slovenia	.682	20	53
Netherlands	.674	19	45
Italy	.644	16	61
Hungary	.626	18	50
Slovakia	.595	21	57
Estonia	.572	22	52
Ireland	.559	20	44
Latvia	.511	22	64
"Rational" economies	**.240**	**21**	**51**
Germany	.473	20	55
France	.398	22	55
Poland	.353	17	62
Denmark	.332	20	49
Finland	.308	21	55
Austria	.168	23	54
Sweden	.145	24	46
Belgium	.140	23	52
Luxembourg	−.153	19	30

consumption in GDP. Two countries not included in our study: Norway (41% consumption and 28% investment in GDP) and Ukraine (71% consumption and 14% investment in GDP) can serve as extreme examples. Unfortunately, we have neither expectation nor external economic data for these countries. The two extremes among European OECD countries are taken by Sweden, Belgium and Luxembourg on the "rational" side and Greece, Portugal and Spain on the "emotional" side (Table 2.5).

Note that "emotional" countries with a low share of investment and a high share of consumption in GDP usually face large economic problems contrary to the more "rational" countries. These proportions can change following political power shifts. A characteristic example is Poland, where the share of consumption increased and the share of investment decreased sharply in 2015–2017, after change of the government. Such a change might announce a drift towards a group of "emotional" countries.

We are dealing with a combination of two axes:

- Dependent vs. independent countries;
- Emotional vs. rational countries.

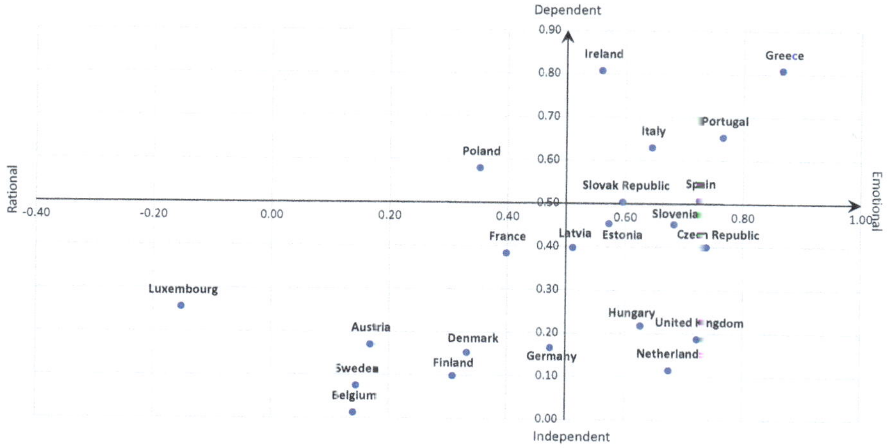

Fig. 2.9 Four types of economies

By crossing these two criteria we are able to identify four types of economies: dependent rational, dependent emotional, independent rational, independent emotional. Each one of the four categories represents different set of policies, different policy windows. This typology is presented on Fig. 2.9. We will discuss each of the categories separately, disregarding the dependent rational field, represented by only one country: Poland, which will be analyzed more in detail in a separate in-depth case study.

The opinion that the political climate plays a key role in the socio-economic dynamics of contemporary modern nation states is generally accepted by social scientists (for example Vogel 2018; Iversen and Soskice 2019; Ward 2015). Changes in socio-economic policies create the political climate, or the other way around: political tinkering builds up policy changes, when the policy window is open. Only the political economy is capable of explaining the real dynamics of socio-economic systems.

In order to incorporate the political factor into our analysis, we have built an political radicalism index based on a simple analysis of the election results between 1999 and 2017. In an attempt to rate the political climate as more or less conducive to economic development and the rational management of the national economy, the following scores were given to the political parties entering parliaments in successive elections, usually taking place every 4 years: center-right 5, center 4, center – left 3, far-right 2 and far-left – 1 By weighing these scores with the participation of parties in national parliaments, we received the "political radicalism index" (Fig. 2.10).

As our analyses demonstrate, European OECD countries gradually became more and more radicalized bending either to the right or to the left. This process accelerated after 2012, i.e. when the last financial crisis ended in Europe. That fact should be further analyzed in different groups of countries (Fig. 2.11).

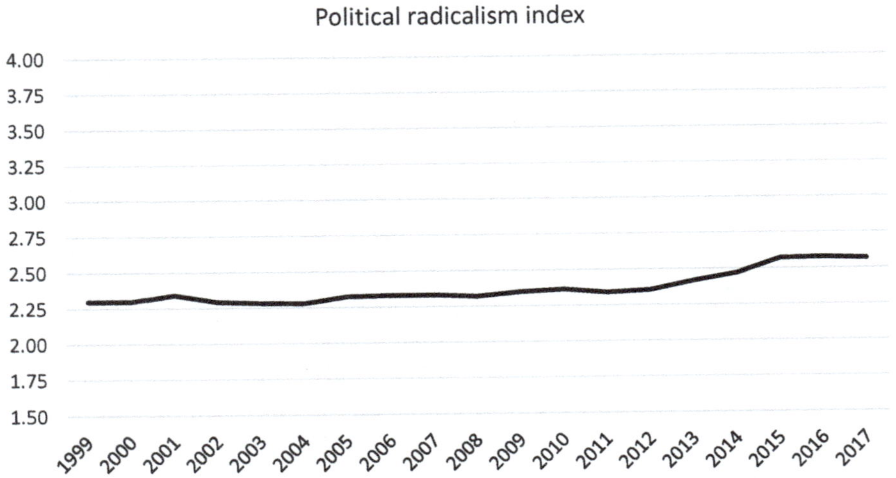

Fig. 2.10 Political radicalism index for 22 OECD European Countries: 1999–2017

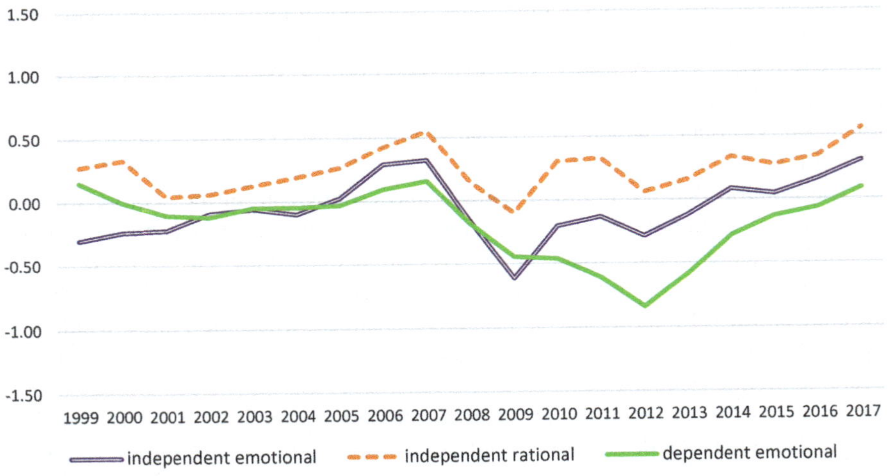

Fig. 2.11 BDI dynamics for three groups of countries, 1999–2017

Let us, however, first compare the BDI changes in rational independent, irrational independent and irrational dependent groups of countries. Irrespective of the changes, the socio-economic development level was the highest in independent rational countries. Independent emotional countries are a bit less developed but since 2001–2017, i.e. during almost the entire period under examination, their BDI value was changing almost exactly the same way as in independent rational countries. The pattern of changes in dependent emotional countries is quite different. In 1999–2001 they were more developed in terms of BDI than independent emotional countries. However, they did not enjoy such a rapid pre-crisis improvement.

Fig. 2.12 Political radicalism index for three groups of countries

Moreover, contrary to other groups, their crisis was continuous from 2008 to 2012, without the short term "mid-crisis" improvement of 2010–2011. Their BDI decline was not only longer but also the most dramatic. That indicates a general weakness of dependent emotional countries which did not enjoy so many benefits in the generally good years and suffered the most during the crisis. All three groups experienced positive BDI dynamics since 2013. All in all, independent rational economies have the highest BDI value and experienced the mildest downturns (Fig. 2.11).

Surprisingly all three groups of countries experience a similar radicalization of the political outlook. The group of dependent emotional countries is particularly interesting from the point of view of the role of political pressure. It contains Greece (the subject of a more detailed study below), Portugal, Italy, Ireland, Spain and Slovakia. This group was the least radical before the crisis but is the most radical after it. Thus, dependent emotional countries were both more affected by the crisis and more emotionally reacted to this crisis after it has ended (Fig. 2.12).

The very notion of a dependent emotional type of economy combines a high degree of dependence on international business, financial and political environment with a high volatility of political mood and an almost hysterical over-reaction of public expectations to changes in socio-economic conditions and to economic policies. This is especially visible in Greece. The BDI value in most of the countries are lower than the European mean. Ireland is the only exception. The crisis has caused BDI changes in this group to be bigger than in Europe as a whole (Fig. 2.13).

Greece, which has suffered a lot during the crisis, reacted to it by the rapid radicalization of politics much more than other dependent emotional countries. Other countries from this group show a higher degree of understanding of the economic mechanisms by public opinion and politicians. The international environment both amplifies and magnifies mistakes and correct choices. If public opinion wants

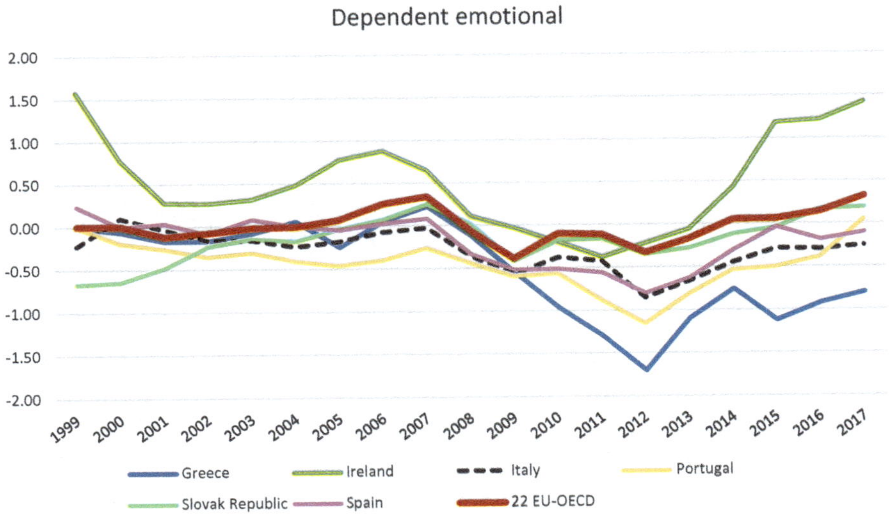

Fig. 2.13 Changes of BDI in dependent emotional countries, 1999–2017

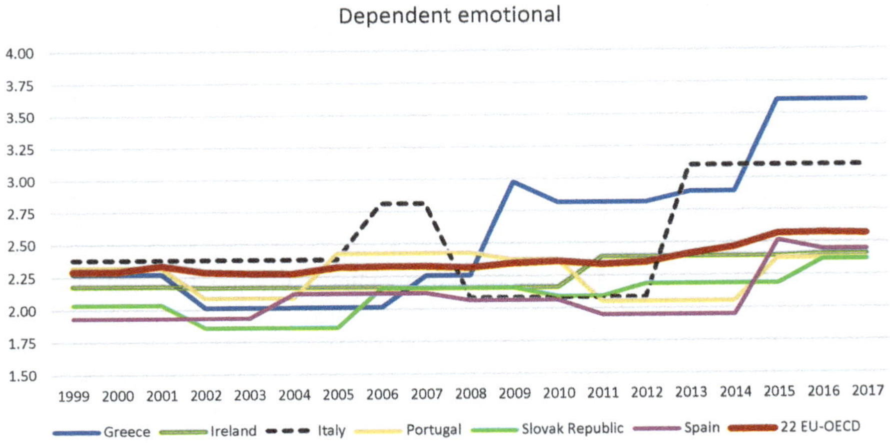

Fig. 2.14 Political radicalism index for dependent emotional countries, 1999–2017

immediate consumption growth, the international environment provides financing at a very high and rapidly growing cost. Financing is made available usually on better terms, if people do not overreact to a slow down or even a decline in consumption and social spending. In the nut shell: "You want it, you get it, but you pay for it". Some of the dependent emotional countries can be compared with reckless debtors taking new cash loans from shady para banks over and over again. The degree of economic education of public opinion and the degree of responsibility of the political class (their ability to resist populist temptations) play a decisive role in this respect.

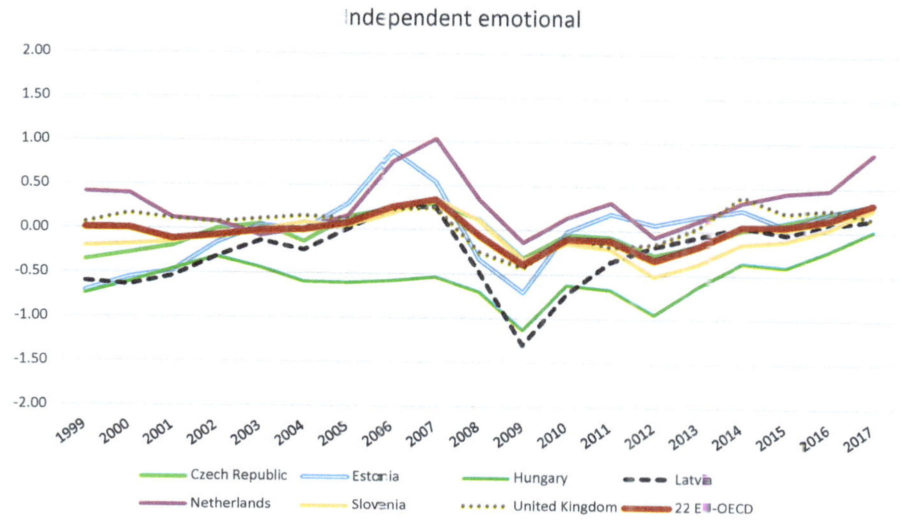

Fig. 2.15 Changes of the BDI in independent emotional countries, 1999–2017

The group of independent emotional countries includes: the Czech Republic, United Kingdom, Hungary, Netherlands, Slovenia, Estonia and Latvia (Fig. 2.15).

The BDI index of independent emotional countries is in some cases lower than the mean for OECD European countries (Hungary), in some case higher (Netherlands) but generally similar to the mean, though also volatile. This may be explained by the combination of outward and inward oriented policies. Such policies are deeply rooted in volatile political processes. Hungary and Latvia suffered the most from the economic crisis, but the time and the pace of their recovery, though on a slightly lower level, doesn't differ much from other countries.

In international economic, financial and business relations these countries run policies of independence and persistent following of national interest, in spite of their small size (Hungary, Slovenia) and unfavorable geo-political location (Latvia, Estonia). This takes place even against mainstream European policies in such areas as the rule of law and immigration (Hungary, Czech Republic) or drug use control (Netherlands). The United Kingdom remains the most conspicuous example of independent rebellious positioning within the EU.

The internal policies of this group of countries are emotional. This means following the public opinion closely and immediately, even if it looks "extravagant" or "strange". The most characteristic example of such stance are: Brexit related policies, or very drastic (almost "cruel") austerity policies introduced in Baltic countries (Latvia, Estonia) in response to 2008 crisis. Here again, the maturity and wisdom of public opinion and political actors, as well as well as the size and structure of resources play a key role, leading to highly divergent outcomes.

One has to notice that the last crisis increased radicalism in Slovenia and in Hungary, the latter being very radical even before. The radicalism of Hungarian politics goes hand in hand with a low BDI level.

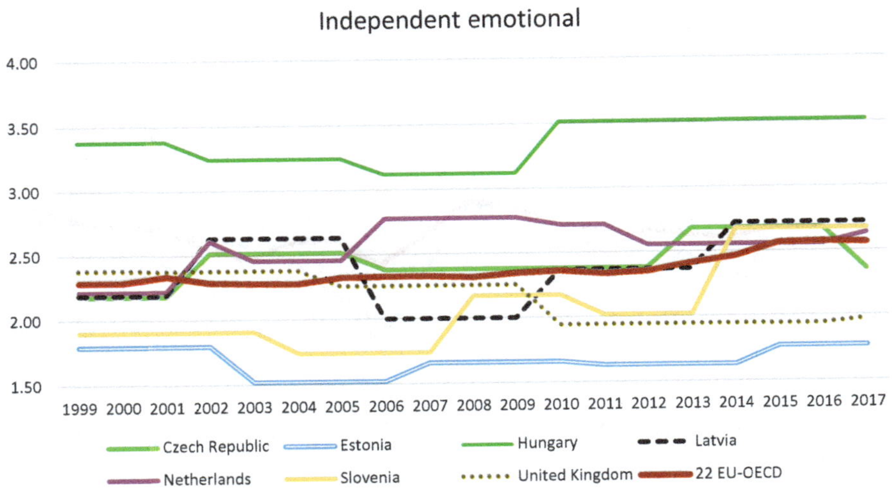

Fig. 2.16 Political radicalism index for independent emotional countries, 1999–2017

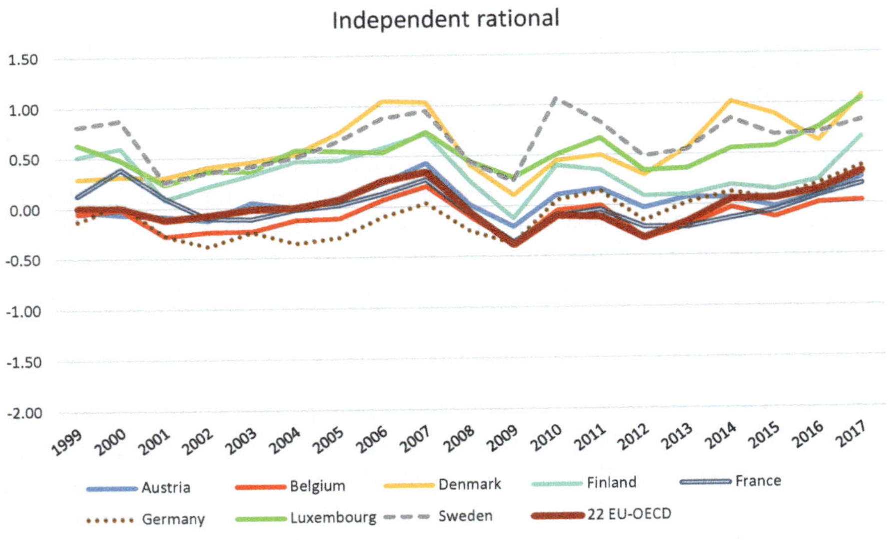

Fig. 2.17 Changes in the BDI in independent rational countries

The group of independent rational countries, the richest ones in our sample, includes Luxemburg, Austria, Sweden, Belgium, Denmark, Finland, Germany and France. They are the countries with a high BDI level. All of them also show the same pattern of BDI changes in time (Fig. 2.17).

Potential for balanced development reforms is not always and not everywhere fully utilized because of political dynamics characterized by mounting radicalism. France, where the necessary reforms of the labor market and social security system

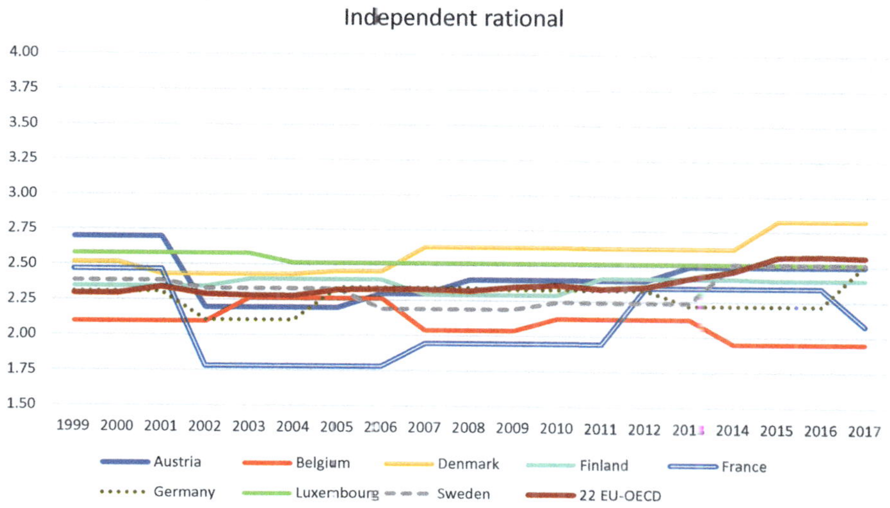

Fig. 2.18 Political radicalism index for independent rational countries, 1999–2017

are successfully blocked by extreme right and extreme left political movements is a characteristic example. Denmark is another example of crisis instigated radicalism (Fig. 2.18).

All independent rational countries have built a solid and versatile welfare state and the rule of law system over the years, enabling to withstand strong political pressures and to give a voice to rational expectations of the large parts of public opinion and moderate political forces. Independence of the rich and basically orderly countries of this group is associated with their attractiveness for international and domestic investors, their competitive advantage on global markets and the scope and strength of international relationships and partnerships. All these are characterized by a high level of competitive advantage (Porter 1990) as compared with other countries included in our sample. Such a privileged position opens a space for rational reforms as in Germany in 2003–2005 (discussed in more detail below).

5 Political Dynamics and BDI

Four groups of countries presented above were identified as Weberian "ideal types", which means that reality is fuzzy and different countries fulfill our criteria of independence and rationality to different degrees. Simplified typologies have their drawbacks that need to be discussed.

Firstly, it is worth noting that many countries are located close to demarcation lines dividing particular groups. For example, Germany is close to the line dividing rational from emotional countries. The German strongest and, according to many, the "healthiest" European economy still remains responsive to social expectations and public opinion claims. This is a sign of reason and moderation. Germany is one of the largest exporters in the world. The resulting dependence upon the external environment is offset by a highly developed "welfare state" and high personal consumption. In such a way, the German economy meets the requirement of "sovereignty" to the extent possible in a globalized world. At the same time, it is "receptive" to social expectations. All four dimensions of social and economic development measured by the BDI (internal and external economic conditions, present social conditions and expectations for the future) remain in dynamic equilibrium called a functional balance. The conclusion: such co-alignment is possible in highly developed economies and mature democracies. The democratic system "harmonizes" the effectiveness of economic management with social expectations providing for controllability and the development of the socio-economic system.

To a different degree, other countries close to the crossroads between ways from dependency to independency and from emotionality to rationality, are approaching this "German model" of moderation. During the 18 years under our investigation, Poland, Latvia, Estonia, France, Slovenia, Slovakia and the Czech Republic demonstrated such behavior. One can wonder whether and to what extent we are dealing with the conscious imitation of Germany by other "countries of the middle", or whether a certain level of dependence on Germany and the necessity of forced adjustments, play a role. France, the second European economy, is competing with Germany without success, but aims at a similar pattern of moderation. It has to be noted that the "yellow vests" movement took place in 2018–2019 beyond our investigation horizon. The presence of post socialist countries in this area of moderation and reason is significant. It confirms the hypothesis of the possibility of successful transformation from plan to market under the umbrella of intense international assistance and strong links with mature international markets and strong liberal democracies. In other words, a unique combination of geopolitical conditions and domestic political situation was needed. Such a window of opportunity was open for a relatively short time (in the 1990s) because of politics. And because of politics it seems closed now.

Relations between the political situation and the course of the business cycle have long been the subject of theoretical research, and Kaldor (1940) was one of the great pioneers of this line of research. At the present time, the relationship between political behavior and political systems on the one side and economic systems and economic performance on the other remains one of the hottest topics in the social sciences touched upon both by leading Marxists including Streeck (2016) and Piketty (2014) and prominent Public Choice theorists such as Buchanan and Tullock (1962). There is an ongoing debate among macroeconomists about the relationship between the business cycle and the political situation. We will return to this topic later on. At this point, however, we can point out that the analysis of the BDI and its components may shed a new light on this subject. The dynamics of all four components of the BDI entails strong interactions between economic policy and politics indispensable for effective system control. Social expectations play a particularly important role. Let us point out first how these expectations and the socio-political situation change.

Our BDI curves analysis shows that the crisis of 2007–2013 led, in a majority of the countries, to very strong slumps in social expectations, exposing the rationality of households to a big test. In many countries it also led to a widespread deterioration of the political climate for economic reforms and the possibility of the real growth of supply factors. Greece and Italy have been the most severely affected by the political climate, but a very significant collapse also occurred in Poland, Hungary, Slovakia, Slovenia, Estonia, Ireland, Spain and Latvia, and Austria, Portugal and even Germany, Sweden and Denmark were also impacted. France defended itself through a deficit in state spending, deteriorating further public finances position and triggering a new wave of unrealistic expectations. A mental and political crisis was avoided in such countries as Luxembourg, Belgium, the Netherlands, Finland, and the Czech Republic. The British political establishment remained formally stable: the Conservative Party did not lose power. Underneath, however, pro Brexit emotions gradually took grip of people's hearts and minds, culminating in the referendum results. Such emotions were rooted in the economic life: inequalities and the poor (below expectations) quality of public services.

Political behavior takes different forms in rational and emotional countries. In the first category, liberal democratic values are embraced by a majority of the voters. In the second, populist and nationalist politicians overwhelm public opinion slipping unrealistic expectations into people's minds and playing "national pride" tunes (along the lines of "America First"), suggesting protectionism and promoting the building of trade and capital flow barriers. Such emotionally underpinned policies inevitably lead to a financial and trade crisis, destroying the chances of rational reforms promoting sustainable and balanced socio-economic development and, in the long run, put the controllability of the system into jeopardy. Hungary provides the most characteristic example of such policies. In recent years, beyond our research time span, Poland also seems to be drifting in this direction. It has to be noted that such emotional policies often enjoy strong and durable political support solidifying power of populist ruling elites, as long as crisis does not hit.

However, the climate and political systems are an epiphenomenon in relation to economic social expectations. It is in the dynamic interaction of social expectations with internal economic factors, corrected by external economic factors, and an ongoing assessment of current social conditions that the functional balance of the system is established. In other words, all four of the BDI dimensions are in a dynamic interplay. Social expectations and social emotions have a decisive, leading role in this process.

6 Controllability and Governability of the System

When analyzing BDI for 22 countries over a relatively long period of time (1999–2017) we have discovered that more "dramatic" (indicating imbalance) changes of BDI curves, expectations curves in particular, are strangely co-variant with political dynamics. In other words, political change (generally bringing about policy shifts and more complex reforms) coexists with the "unusual" rise of

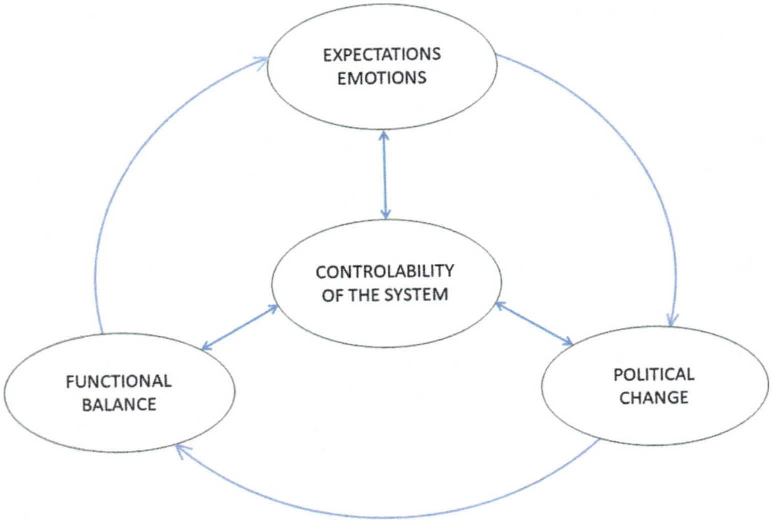

Fig. 2.19 Controllability of the system

expectations. This brings about the emotional dimension of economic life and policy changes generally overlooked and underestimated in the literature of economics and economic sociology (Fig. 2.19).

This is certainly an over-simplifying picture. In order to better explain the role emotions and other components of the BDI in the dynamics of development, one should take into consideration the balance between them, or in other words, the degree of harmony between the external and internal economic conditions, social expectations and current social conditions into consideration. This is statistically measured by standard deviation (Fig. 2.20).

Our analysis shows that independent rational countries are characterized by a higher level of imbalance than other countries. In simple words, this means that rational policy making is usually accompanied by a certain degree of disequilibrium. One can risk a hypothesis that disequilibrium stimulates policy changes firstly in rational countries, but also sometimes in emotional ones when they embark on reforms path (Fig. 2.21).

As we will demonstrate below, reforms were undertaken in conditions of imbalance between the four components of the BDI.

Two more meaningful conclusions can be drawn from the standard deviation analysis:

- Changes in standard deviation curves are preceded by emotional social expectations for the future;
- Expectation curves reach their highs in the best and the worst of times (in terms of a general socio-economic climate).

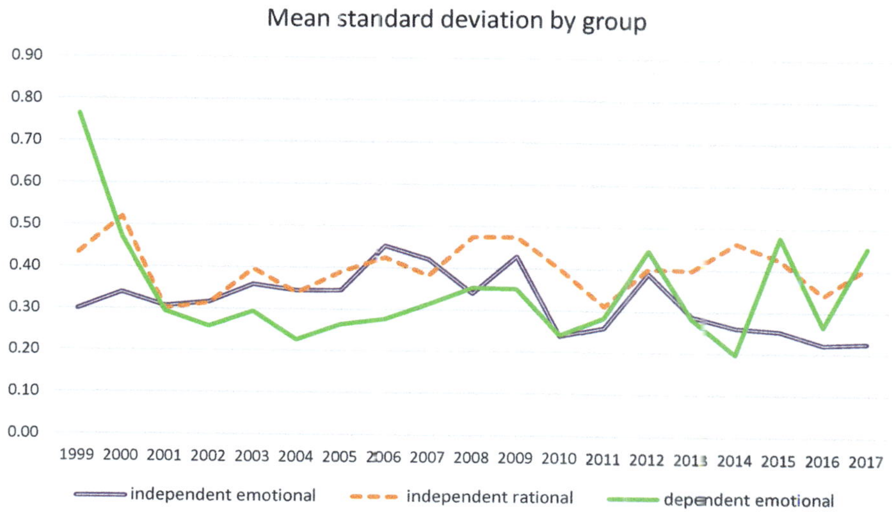

Fig. 2.20 Mean standard deviation between four middle-level BDI indices by group of countries

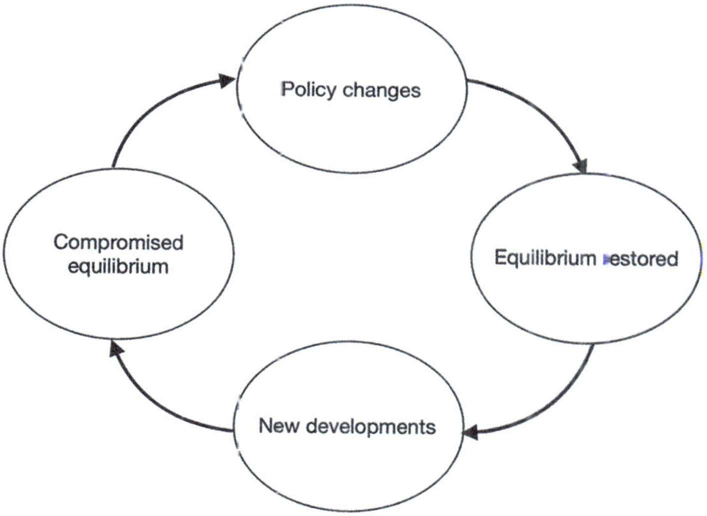

Fig. 2.21 Equilibrium and policy making

Economic policies are, to a great extent, emotionally driven. In order to explain this in more detail, megatrends and policies of specific countries have to be brought into the picture.

Chapter 3
Successful and Unsuccessful Reforms: Germany, Greece and Spain

1 Special Socio-Economic Reforms in Germany in 1999–2017

Our data on socio-economic development allow the special cases of Germany, Spain and Greece to be examined. In all these countries reforms were undertaken to restore compromised equilibria. Germany provides the most spectacular example of a successful reform (Fig. 3.1).

At the beginning of the analyzed period, Germany was characterized by a low rate of economic growth, the average of which was 1.6% in 1995–2001, well below the average for the EU countries. Throughout the last decade of the 20th century, the GDP in Germany grew by only 18% when, for example, in the Netherlands growth reached 34% and, in the UK, even 35%, thanks to the neoliberal reforms introduced in the 1980s by M. Thatcher. In 2002, unemployment in Germany reached a record level of 13.4 (6.9% in the West and 18.6% in the East). The general outlook of internal economic factors was clearly negative. Despite the high unemployment rate, the demand for jobs, the willingness to work by German citizens was low and German entrepreneurs sought labor abroad. At the same time German investment abroad (FDI) increased sharply. Such a situation was interpreted in the neo-liberal literature as resulting from an excess of welfare state protection (high social and unemployment benefits) and a disproportionally high standard of living as compared with productivity growth. Germany acquired the reputation of a country with the highest labor costs (Krebs and Scheffel 2013; Kluve and Jacobi 2006).

Our analysis of the BDI curve and its four components shows, however, that the situation was much more complex. Certainly, the socio-economic balance analyzed by the BDI was disrupted in 2003, 2009 and 2012 mostly due to deteriorating social expectations, which were relatively low in Germany in other times as well. The state

A. K. Koźmiński et al., *The Balanced Development Index for Europe's OECD Countries, 1999–2017*, SpringerBriefs in Economics,
https://doi.org/10.1007/978-3-030-39240-6_3

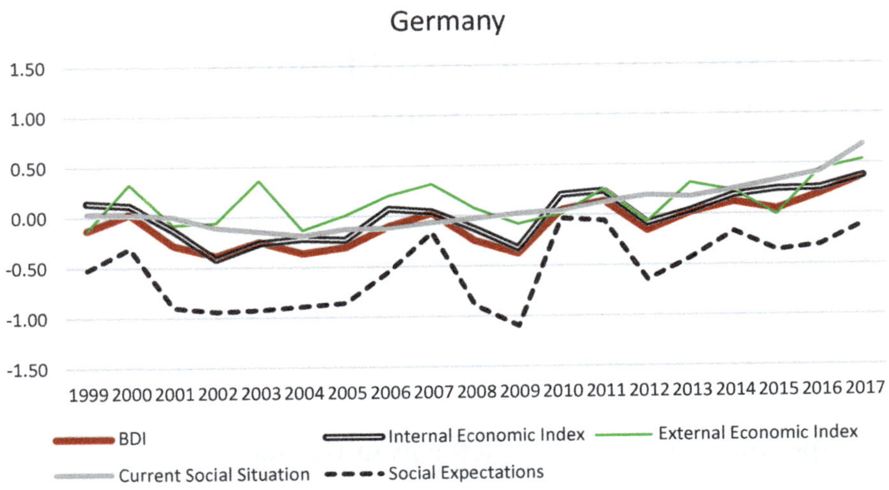

Fig. 3.1 Germany's BDI and its four components

was losing control of the system and social expectations were already very volatile. However, the German BDI seemed to be affected by the financial crisis less than in most other countries. Moreover, the general outlook indicates its almost consistent growth since 2003, with very short lasting and not very deep declines in 2008–2009 and 2012. Nevertheless, the current social situation was not affected by the crisis and seemed to satisfy the Germans thanks to a comfortable safety nest provided by the generous welfare state. Social conditions were improving during the crisis and are currently better than the situation in other domains. Relatively low social expectations, resulting more from the costs of German reunification than from unfavorable income-productivity ratios, gave an opportunity to carry out difficult economic reforms, above all in the labor market. Expectations and consumption aspirations were somehow calmed by the overall sensation of crisis and the reunification of the country. The deterioration of social expectations did not precede the crisis but was concurrent with it.

Unemployment benefits were really impressive in Germany at the beginning of the 21st century. People losing their jobs had a guaranteed 67% of the last wage (the maximum, however, was EUR 4250 if they had children, and 60% without children.). After this period, they were granted unemployment assistance at the level of the 57% of the last wage (with children) or 53% (without children) unlimited in time. Such an evident socialist generosity had enormous micro and macroeconomic effects. The transformation of a large number of workers from the German Democratic Republic into this extraordinarily generous social security system threatened not only to maintain high unemployment, but also created a risk of strong macroeconomic imbalance, high budget deficits and public debt. Such social security system was generally accepted by a majority of Germans and the German economy was capable of maintaining it without compromising the well-being of people during the reunification and even during the last financial crisis. This resulted in a disproportionally high value of the current social conditions index at the beginning and after the end of the last crisis.

After reunification of West and East Germany, the real danger of system abuse and its excessively high cost became clearly evident. Social, political and economic tensions increased and something needed to be done about it, if the German economy was to maintain its leading position in Europe and in the world and maintain the high level of well-being of the citizens.

The Social Democratic Chancellor of Germany (1998–2005), G. Schröder, faced the urgent necessity of neoliberal labor market reforms. A special commission, headed by Peter Hartz, Volkswagen's HR director, proposed four stages of labor market reforms. Following the Hartz Commission's recommendations, special legislation called the "Laws for Reform of the Job Market," (or Hartz Reforms) was enacted between January 2003 and January 2005. These new laws included:

1. Creation of a Personal-Service-Agentur to act as temporary agencies to match unemployed people with employers. This new law was aimed at increasing the effectiveness and efficiency of labor market services and at implementing policies of re-organization of the local employment agencies. Such agencies were, in principle, market driven.
2. A new grant for entrepreneurs, known as the "Ich-AG" (Me, Inc.) was aimed at encouraging the creation of new businesses.
3. Unemployment benefits were cut by up to 30% if a person refused to take up a reasonable job offer. Special measures aimed at activating the unemployed were introduced in order to encourage proactive behavior of the unemployed and to increase active labor force share among the entire adult population.
4. Social welfare and unemployment benefits were merged in order to foster the employment demand. Deregulation of the temporary work sector followed. Exemptions from restrictions on fix-term contracts and the loosening of dismissal protection provided for linking the labor market with a competition driven free market economy (see: Kluve and Jacobi 2006).

The above reforms have not only brought about significant changes in the approach to the labor market, but also a change in the relations between the four regulators of the economy: households – enterprises – markets – the state (Noga 2016). Harmonizing household interests as consumers, employees, entrepreneurs and citizens Hartz-Schroeder reforms were also aimed at public administration reinforcing the rules of decentralized entrepreneurial management.

Between 2007 and 2008, the unemployment rate in Germany fell to 7.5%, and during the global crisis only slightly increased. The reformed German labor market demonstrated its ability to reach the unemployment level of only 5.5% in 2012. Econometric research shows that a three percentage point decline of unemployment and the creation of 2.5 million jobs can be attributed to the Hartz-Schroder reforms (Gaskarth 2014). The international competitiveness of Germany has also increased enormously.

All this resulted in internal economic conditions being worse than external conditions till 2009, exceeding them after the crisis.

In many other countries, particularly in France, similar reforms were attempted. However, the resistance of the French society and, above all, the trade unions' negative power were insurmountable. Despite this fact, France's attempts to implement labor market reforms brought some partial success under the presidency of E. Macron. They were not bold enough to close the growing gap between the economic performance of Germany and France, though France was most of the time better off in terms of general BDI.

The success of P. Hartz's reforms was possible thanks to the very strong political and pragmatic determination of G. Schroder, a neo-socialist undertaking neoliberal solutions. That confirms the merit of "new pragmatism" in socio-economic policies (Kołodko 2017). Speaking in terms of the BDI, the Hartz Commission wanted to improve the socio-economic balance and controllability of the system. The commission consisted of 15 members, including: two representatives of the world of science, two trade unionists, one representative of employers, representatives of consulting companies, business and government administration. It was a rather technocratic undertaking lacking strong support from a political party.

In spite of the unquestionable success of labor market reforms the social democratic administration of Chancellor Schroeder suffered political defeat in the general election of 2005 (see Fig. 3.2). At the end of the second decade of the 21st century, the benefits of the Hartz-Schroder reforms may no longer be sufficient for the German economy to maintain its comparative global competitive advantage. The economic performance of this country may be very strongly affected by strong political turbulence in international trade, primarily in the US and China "trade war", carrying a risk for German exports. The middle level index of German external economic functioning fell below the internal one in 2012–2014. If Germany is to

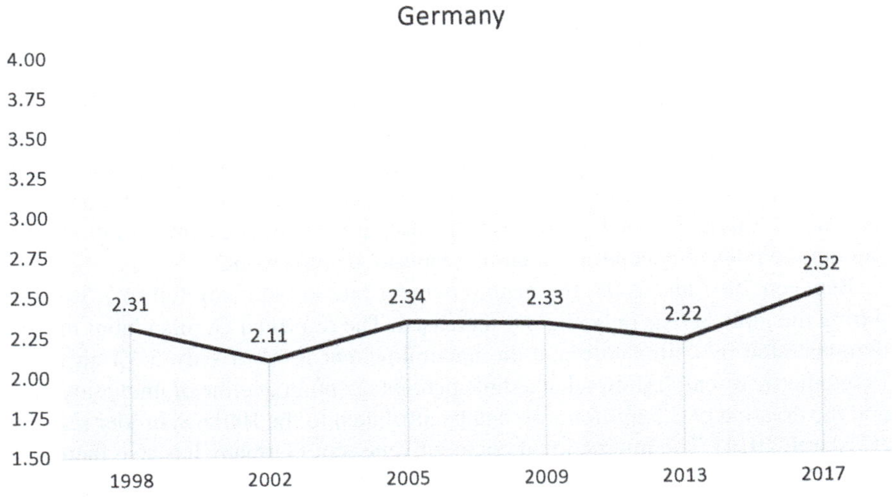

Fig. 3.2 Germany's political radicalism index

maintain its leading position, a new wave of socio-economic reforms will be needed. According to our model, Germany is well positioned for new reforms, due to the high level of the BDI index and a relatively low level of imbalance between its four main components: external and internal economic conditions, current social conditions and expectations for the future. The apparent radicalization of politics may have a negative effect, though.

2 Greek Tragedy

Failed attempts to reform the Greek economy are portrayed in abundant economic literature as a "Greek tragedy" (see Galbraith 2016; Varoufakis 2017; Blanchard 2015 among others) or even – alluding to the famous line from the "Zorba the Greek" movie – as a "beautiful catastrophe" (Kołodko 2016). The Greek case provides convincing evidence that politics matter for development no less than emotions and underlying social consciousness. Our analysis of the BDI index combined with a simplified retrospective of political dynamics clearly confirm such a conviction. The deterioration of the Greek external economic conditions, triggered by the 2008 subprime crisis (which became apparent a year earlier than in most other countries and was continuously worsening for 4 years) was accompanied by pessimistic expectations and deterioration of the internal economic conditions. However, due to, among others, the continuation of an excessive welfare policy and tax avoidance, the current social conditions started to very slowly deteriorate only 2 years later and then remained at almost the same level until 2016–2017, when internationally enforced austerity measures started to affect the people. The importance of international economic and political pressure has been clearly indicated by a drastic deterioration of the functioning of the Greek economy in international surroundings. The middle-level index of the economy's external functioning was the most affected by a crisis in Greece, while social expectations were most affected in a majority of the other countries. In Greece, the curve illustrating economic external factors is falling dramatically during the crisis, showing how the country conducting a bad economic internal policy it is exposed to a catastrophe when external factors worsen. Politically, the Greek crisis was accompanied by a continuous evolution towards more radical (leftist) forms of government. Such a political situation made the reforms even more difficult (Fig. 3.4).

The roots of the Greek drama can be attributed to turbulent modern history on the outskirts of Europe. During World War II Greece experienced brutal German occupation confronted by the strong popular resistance movement and legendary partisan struggle. German occupation was followed by a civil war between communists supported by the Soviet Union and pro-western forces. The newly established democracy was interrupted by the CIA backed "black colonels" coup of 1967. Democracy was finally restored in 1974. The tradition of the highly divisive, emotional Greek politics fueled by a generally low standard of living and high inequalities is well entrenched. Throughout its history, Greece was always highly

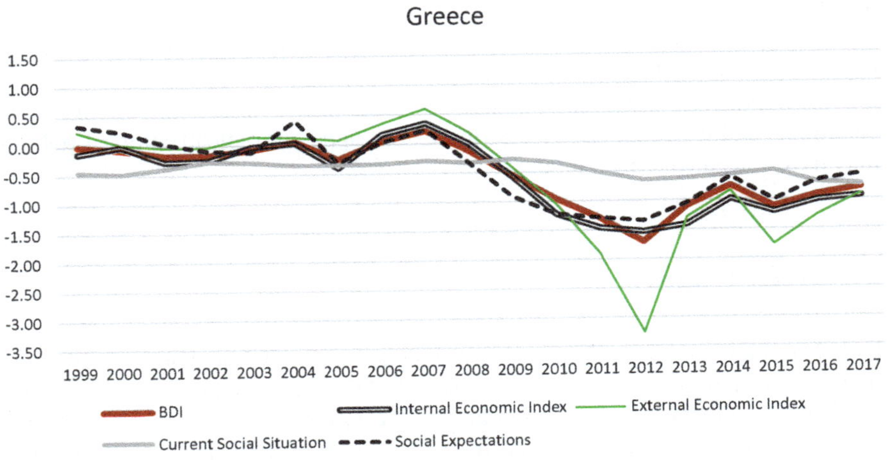

Fig. 3.3 Greece's BDI and its four components

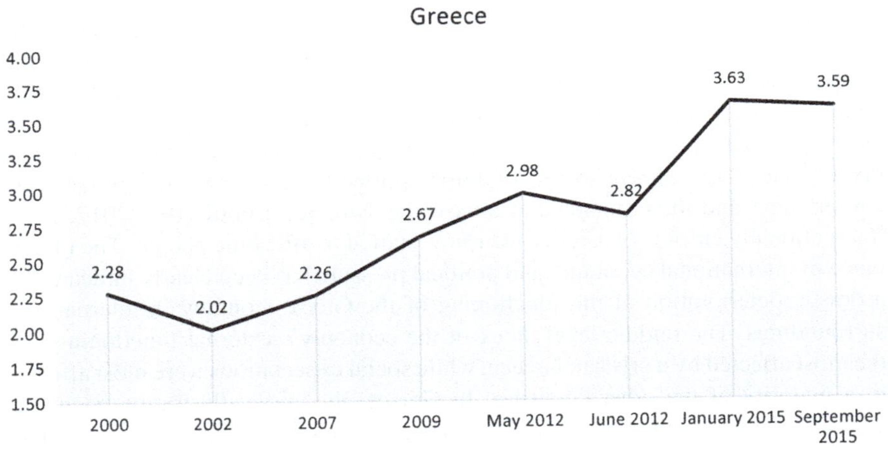

Fig. 3.4 Greece's political radicalism index

dependent upon the international economic and political environment and around 2010 it triggered the Greek crisis.

Greece was admitted into the eurozone in 2001 for political reasons in spite of the generally known and obvious weaknesses of its economy and overly high government spending financed by external debt. That resulted in the improvement in Greek politics in 2002, which was a subject of almost constant radicalization later on (Fig. 3.5).

The Greek government was always a heavy borrower. It is commonly known truth that the country had an overly large civil service, too generous and often abused pension plans and social services, patronage based politics, aggressive

Fig. 3.5 Greece's public debt (% of GDP)

unions, dubious accounts. Moreover, tax evasion was the most popular national sport. The economy itself was relatively weak and technologically not advanced, except for tourism and the maritime sector. Creditors knew it, nevertheless they kept on lending money. Already in 2010, the level of Greek debt exceeded its total GDP. This situation was typical for the then unbalanced euro zone including richer and poorer countries, fiscally prudent and fiscally unstable ones. In such a system, one country's deficit becomes another country's surplus. More advanced euro countries (such as Germany, Netherlands or Austria) of highly competitive export industries needed peripheral countries like Greece to serve as outlets for massive inflows of imports and convenient investment locations (both FDI and short term speculative). In the case of Greece, this international imbalance was pushed to the extreme, due to an excessive disproportion of competitiveness between the Greek economy and the most advanced economies of the euro zone.

The economic imbalance, however, was not easily observable by the general public and even by the economists, some of whom accused the Greek authorities of rigging the statistics. Since 2010, the Greek budget deficit was officially only at the level of about .2% of the GDP of the European Union (Kołodko 2016: 40). The situation changed when the American subprime crisis hit Europe. The time of disclosing the cards and scrutiny of debt-based assets came. Several large European banks found themselves in possession of doubtful poisoned assets including Greek government papers. At that moment, Greece was declared close to bankruptcy, and much larger economies of the south of Europe (covered by the acronym PIGS: Portugal, Italy, Greece and Spain) were found on shaky grounds. Shareholders of big ("too big to fail") Western European banks badly needed some kind of rescue plan. Such a plan had to meet two essential conditions: to shift the risk from private to public agents and to avoid the danger of eventual debt forgiveness of other PIGS.

The series of "assistance" plans for Greece met both criteria. The plans agreed between "troika" (European Commission, European Central Bank and International Monetary Fund) and consecutive Greek governments consisted of several waves of debt financing and hard austerity plans imposed on the Greek economy. In such a way, the Greek debt became an obligation to public organizations represented by "troika" and ultimately to EU taxpayers. The Greek debt rose to over 180% of the GDP in 2016 and became obviously unpayable regardless of the repayment period. But debt forgiveness was not declared and a dangerous precedent was not set. Austerity measures imposed on Greece were needed to legitimize lending to bankrupt state borrowers in the eyes of public opinion of the richest euro zone countries, Germany in particular. At the same time, these measures completely ruined the Greek economy and hurt the Greek population. It also deprived the Greek government of the "financial space" necessary to implement the so badly needed reforms of the weak (undercapitalized) and corrupt banking system, inefficient public administration, taxation system, wasteful pension and social security system, restructuring or privatization of state owned companies etc. However, as BDI components indicate, the current social conditions were still better than it could have been provided deterioration of both external and internal economic conditions. Social gains achieved by people are difficult to be quickly and drastically reduced.

Greece was pushed by outside political forces into the syndrome of the "triple 25":

- Over 25% recession since 2010;
- Over 25% unemployment rate;
- 25% of the population living below the threat of poverty level (Kołodko 2016: 46).

The total cost of "assistance" producing such triple results is staggering – EUR 326 billion, i.e. the largest bailout fund ever. It was designated to a small country of just 11 million inhabitants. At present, the Greek GDP (PPP) amounts to only .25% of the total world production and less than 1.5% of the GDP of the EU (28 countries, before Brexit). It is obvious that "troika" knew perfectly well that the Greek debt will be never paid-off, the imposed austerity measures will further destroy the already weak economy and will block the necessary reforms (Varoufakis 2015). Nevertheless, the "troika" used all the political pressure and economic blackmail instruments to impose three consecutive bailout deals on Greece. The last one, worth EUR 43 billion, is scheduled to end of 2019 leaving Greece as an impoverished peripheral country, a victim of both its own errors and pan-European politics.

In exchange for EUR 326 billion, consecutive Greek governments had to implement 10 economic recovery plans and undertook hundreds different savings programs such as wage and salary freezes, reduction of pensions, increases of retirement age, privatization programs, liberalization of energy and labor markets etc. (Le Monde, 12/12/2015). Reforms were half-hearted and the results were meager due to the basic structural weaknesses of the economy and persistent resistance of both the corrupt elites and desperate population.

A comprehensive and bold reform was blocked from abroad, but internal politics had their share as well. The impoverished and hopeless population supported both left and right extremist political forces. Ultimately, the leftist Syriza party came to power in 2015. The necessary reforms were blocked consistently with the dominating populist political inclinations. The resistance concerned in particular: privatization, taxation and social welfare. External and internal political forces contributed jointly to the Greek drama of impossible reform. Emotions of the frugal northerners afraid of paying the "lazy southerners", combined with the vested interests of the financial establishment and European politics prevailed over basic economic rationality, producing a self-defeating monster worth more than 320 billion Euro in one of the smallest and less advanced EU countries.

3 Controversies around Spanish Reforms

As the analysis of the BDI curve shows, Spain is a highly emotional country. The curve of social expectations shows high volatility. It was disproportionally high at the turn of the century and fell until 2005, despite the constant slow improvement of three other BDI domains. The short pre-crisis period of 2006–2007 was characterized by an apparent but not a very big improvement in all four domains, expectations included. The expectations deteriorated much more than other also deteriorating aspects in 2008 in result of the first news on the world financial crisis. Thus, the overoptimism turned into overpessimism. Undoubtedly, the initial overoptimism, though declining, resulted from the strong dependence of the Spanish economy not only on international trade, foreign capital inflows (EU funds included) and tourism, but upon intellectual input improving financial and business models and pragmatics. All of them were improving. Several leading business universities in Spain have become the best in the world, modelled after American universities and competing effectively with them. The fact that social expectations were declining in Spain for a relatively long time while external economic conditions were imrpoving may deserve a more detailed study. That might have happened because external economic conditions improved faster than current social conditions and, especially, internal economic situation.

Spanish financial markets experienced a huge construction bubble similar to the American insolvency trap. It resulted in dramatic credit expansion following the 2007 Wall Street model. Between 1996 and 2007, the share of credit in the GDP increased from 70% to 180%. Due to the strong links between Spanish and American banks and financial institutions, the Spanish economy was rapidly and dramatically infected with the 2007 financial decease and all four of the BDI domains deteriorated, social expectations the most. The political slide towards more radical forms of government followed after 2011 (Figs. 3.6 and 3.7).

The crisis of 2008–2013 led to reduced financial and economic activity in Spain. A raft of economic stimulus measures were adopted to counter this situation. The lack of positive results from those measures, a worsening of the international

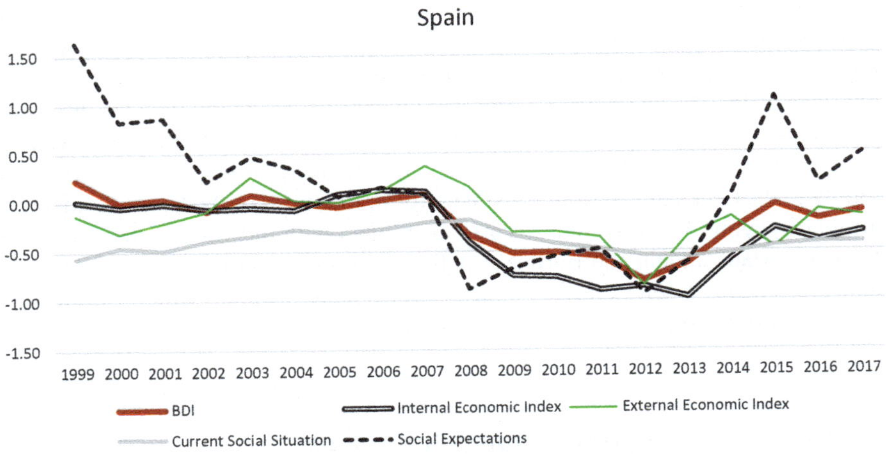

Fig. 3.6 Spain's BDI and its four components

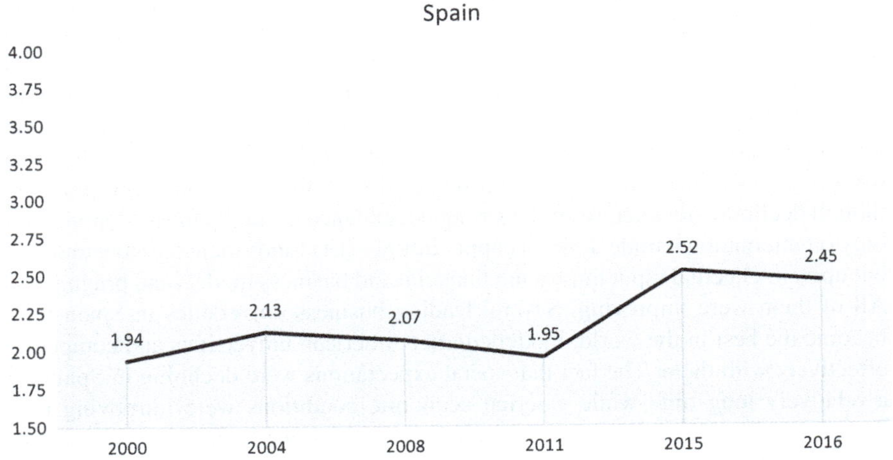

Fig. 3.7 Spain's political radicalism index

financial crisis and the absence of new, more effective economic measures led to an overall deterioration that is reflected in the following figures:

- A sharp decline in economic activity: from the GDP growth of 3.6% in 2007 to −3.7% in 2009; −0.1% in 2010; 0.4% in 2011; and a −1.7% in 2012.
- A high rate of unemployment: from 8.6% of the workforce in 2007 to 22.5% in 2011 and 24.6% at the 2012.
- A concurrent reduction in tax revenue and an increase in public spending, which led to a public deficit of 8.9% of GDP in 2011 (from a public account surplus equal to 1.9% of GDP in 2007).

- An increase in the public debt-to-GDP ratio from 40.2% in 2008 to as much as 68.5% at the end of 2011 and 72.1% in June 2012 (Gobierno de Espana, Minsterio de la Presidencia 2012).

As of 2010, the government was forced to start reducing public spending, while in many countries, led by the US, the Keynesian stimulation of the economy by a quantitative easing and high deficits continued. In Spain, wages have been frozen, public sector salaries cut by 5%, and other important measures taken in order to limit public spending. In 2010, the tripartite negotiations over the labor market took place. The collective bargaining structure was decentralized, allowing companies to derogate wages at the plant-level and set working conditions through negotiation processes. All these have resulted in some deterioration of the current social and economic conditions.

The program of overcoming the 2008–13 crisis included a mix of different economic measures. On the one hand, the measures related to interference and huge financial support from the state and "troika" (IMF, World Bank, ECB) resulted in an increase of the public debt. On the other hand, a long "neoliberal" cleansing of the economy with very high unemployment, painful restructuring of the business and, above all, a strong budget cuts had moderating effects. The mix also included institutional reforms, especially the labor and social market. They were not as radical as Hartz-Schroder's reforms, although considered by many analysts more effective and far reaching than in France or Italy. It must also be admitted that a very good international, business climate helped tremendously in the 2014–2017 period. These measures resulted in substantial concurrent improvement in all fours developmental domains after 2013, the greatest in social expectations.

The OECD commends the Spanish government for having introduced "an impressive range of reforms to improve the labor market, enhance the fiscal framework, tackle long-standing education and housing issues, and improve the business environment". According to the OECD study, only Greece and Ireland have done more to reform their economies than Spain, and only Greece and Portugal have cut their public deficits more radically than Spain (OECD 2018).

The reform process itself aroused several controversies. The unemployment increase was shocking. When the housing sector collapsed in 2008, Spain entered a deep recession that contrasted starkly with the glaring performance of the previous years. At that time, the labor market was characterized by a widespread use of fixed term contracts. In effect of the liberalization of labor market in the 1980s (much earlier than the time-span of our analyses), fixed term contracts already constituted close to 90% of the new contracts in the 1990s (Dolado et al. 2002). When the crisis hit, the highly flexible workforce shrank dramatically, being responsible for 52% of the total loss of jobs all over Europe (de Bustillo and Anton 2015). It's no wonder that the current social conditions improved in post-crisis Spain slower than in the three other domains of development.

The dramatic labor market collapse and neoliberal measures taken by the government led to a similarly dramatic change in the political climate between 2011 and 2015. Nevertheless, the government elected earlier on the wave of protest against neoliberal policies was forced to carry them on. Under the influence of international financial institutions, the left-wing government led by José Luis Zapatero (PSOE) continued the austerity measures and labor market deregulation despite trade unions resistance.

Finally the government of J. L. Zapatero had to operate under contradicting pressures from the troika and international financial institutions on one side and a dissatisfied population as well as powerful trade unions on the other. Before the departure, however, it even managed to change the Constitution, introducing the principle of maintaining the country's fiscal stability in accordance with the ECB's recommendations.

At the end of 2011, the government was taken over by the new right-wing government, of Mariano Rajoy. Since 2012 this government carried out another radical reform of the labor market. It was introduced rather brutally without negotiations, consultation or social dialogue with the opposition parties. As part of the reform, priority was given to labor negotiations at the enterprise level. The collective bargaining privilege was limited to 2 years and compensation for unfair dismissal reduced. In addition, in 2016, the government reduced CIT taxation from 30% to 25%. These reforms were very positively received by the troika and very badly by employees, trade unions and even by the ILO, which usually attempts to harmonize the interests of the employees, employers and government. Nevertheless, the reforms began to bring positive changes in the economy: revival, an increase in the competitiveness of Spanish enterprises considerably increased the efficiency of operations.

Critics of the reform, however, point out that the social price of these positive effects was definitely too high, and on the other, that positive changes in the Spanish economy were not so much the result of these reforms, but were mostly due to the overall external improvement of the global and European economy, the positive impact of the weakening of the euro on Spanish exports, the fall of oil prices and the improved economic climate in the US. Thus, the controversies surrounding reforms in the Spanish did not differ from the most general, widespread controversy in economic theory and policy.

There is no doubt that economic cycles and attempts to regulate them by policy and economic reforms can be better understood thanks to the BDI, particularly its middle-level components, rather than by analyzing the GDP alone and other "hard" business indicators. This is particularly visible on the example of the Spanish economy. In an emotional and dependent country one has to take the leading role of social expectations and external economic conditions into consideration. They contribute to the cycle alongside classical and neoclassical supply factors, such as labor, capital and technical progress, as well as political factors.

Despite quite different changes in the four middle-level indices of the four developmental domains, the Spanish overall BDI index remained practically unchanged in the period preceding the crisis, i.e. between 1999 and 2007. It remained relatively stable irrespective of the fact that Spain experienced a strong speculative "bubble" in the real estate market and a huge increase in speculative credit in the economy artificially improving the economic climate for a short time.

But this short time improvement concerned only a relatively small part of the society: the upper and upper middle class, the majority felt little progress. The deterioration of social expectations were observed in time of the "big boom" at the beginning of the 21st century, as shown by Spain's BDI figure. The curve of social expectations has been dropping consistently since 1999, not growing between 2003 and 2007 despite the rising indices of internal and external economic conditions. The greater part of the society definitely noticed somewhat of an artificial nature of the prosperity. The majority of the population was definitively politically leaning towards the left. More recently neoliberals from modern business schools lost their influence in intellectual circles, and the left wing movements invite such economic advisors as T. Piketty or J. Galbraith. The curve of social expectations is recently going up faster than three other curves. Will such trend bring about an economic recovery consuming the results of difficult reforms, or will it result in imposing populist policies? This is one of the most interesting dilemmas of the contemporary socio-economic theory and policy.

Chapter 4
In-Depth Case Study: Poland

1 Poland as Transition Economy

Poland is the only one of the Central European post-communist (or rather the so called post-"real socialism") countries, which experienced a deep and rapid transition shock after the fall of the Soviet Empire as early as in 1989, but was quickly considered a very successful transition country, until 2015 at least. Nevertheless, some specific features of Polish "real socialism" should be brought up in order to explain transition process and further developments.

- In the case of Poland history matters. As a result of consecutive, sometimes bloody riots against the regime (1956, 1970, 1976, 1981), Poland enjoyed the most liberal and permissive version of a socialist regime and was the only country in the Soviet bloc in which the non-communist political and intellectual elite existed and was ultimately *de-facto* recognized by the communists as a "round table" negotiation partner in 1989. A peaceful and relatively smooth political transition towards democracy followed.
- In the 1970s, Poland went through an intensive (and impressive at the beginning) "socialist modernization" period based on massive imports of western technology financed by foreign debt. The inefficient and wasteful economy did not produce a sufficient return on ambitious projects and the total bankruptcy of the country followed. Nevertheless, massive exposure to the West and the relative freedom to travel had a powerful impact on people's mentality and personal wealth in hard currency accumulated through the illegal work of millions of Polish "tourists" in the US and Western Europe. On top of that the Polish academics (particularly in such fields as: economics, finance management, social sciences etc.) were offered generous scholarships, financing prolonged study visits of the top universities of the Western world (mainly in the US).

A. K. Koźmiński et al., *The Balanced Development Index for Europe's OECD Countries, 1999–2017*, SpringerBriefs in Economics,
https://doi.org/10.1007/978-3-030-39240-6_4

- In the last months of "real socialism", Poland had by far the largest private sector in the Soviet bloc. In 1980 16.6% of the GDP came from the private sector, in 1989 it was 19.2%. Over 90% of the agricultural land was in private hands (Brieitkopf et al. 1991; Cassell and Cichy 1987). In the 1970s, Polish citizens were allowed to hold bank accounts in hard currency. In addition, an estimated over USD 2 billion was kept in cash "under the mattresses" of private citizens. Such hard currency reserves constituted private cushions against shocks. They were available to a relatively large population and could be used as seed money for entrepreneurial startups.
- Starting from anti-Stalinist "October revolution" in 1956, Poland went through a series of unsuccessful, but highly instructive reforms and experiments aimed at decentralization and marketization of the economy. Reforms were broadly discussed among professional economists and the general public. These discussions led to the generally assumed conclusion that the rational, efficient allocation of resources was not possible in a centrally planned economy, and only the "real market" was able to provide satisfactory solutions (Koźmiński 1988, 2008).
- Since the 1956 "Poznan June", Poland developed a tradition of workers' militancy, the most fully embodied in 10 million members strong "Solidarity" free trade union in 1980. This tradition was inherited by some other civic movements, such as the contemporary women's rights mobilization or coal miners' resistance against mine closings.

Due to inefficient economy, political tensions and intensity of "Solidarity" led political struggle against the regime imposed and supported by Moscow, the situation in Poland could only be described as catastrophic at the starting point of the transition (fall of 1989), even as compared to other countries of the socialist bloc. Inflation exceed 260% in 1989 and 400% in 1990. The population experienced shortages of the most basic administratively low priced foodstuffs in the state owned stores, while the black market flourished. People were desperate. The GDP per capita amounted to only half of Czechoslovakia's GDP. The Polish state was technically bankrupt. The total income from meagre exports, mainly to "socialist bloc" countries, which amounted to only USD 16 billion (from nation in the center of Europe with a population of 38 million!), did not allow to pay the interest on the foreign debt. Subsistence agriculture employed a quarter of the workforce. Infrastructure was one of the worst in Europe (Piatkowski 2018: 126–127). Poland was generally perceived as a future looser in the transition race. Sovietologists and other experts were betting on Hungary or even Ukraine to win.

Poland unexpectedly became an unrivalled transition leader not only among the peers from the region but worldwide. Between 1989 and 2017 Poland's per capita GDP almost tripled in PPP terms reaching USD 27,000. Poland achieved a high income country status the fastest among its global peers, just behind the previous record of South Korea. After reaching the upper middle income threshold of USD 10,000 (World Bank standard) it took just 15 years to achieve high income status crossing the "middle income trap", generally feared by experts, with stellar speed.

It has grown without interruption between 1992 and 2019, i.e. 27 years in a row, beating the historical records of South Korea, Singapore and Japan. Already in 2016, Poland's individual consumption crossed 70% of the euro zone. The same year, the income from exports (mainly to the EU countries) exceeded the amount of USD 250 billion. Poland's distance to the West has never been closer (Piatkowski 2018). International financial institutions agree that Poland's transition from a centrally planned to a market economy was practically completed in the middle of the 1990s (EBRD 1996).

Let us recall the multi-phase model of transition from a planned to a market economy (Koźmiński 1993: 3–4) in order to explain Poland's success. It is composed of several steps:

- The political phase consisting in the elimination of communist domination, consolidation of a democratic electoral system, political parties and democratic institutions (including judiciary) came about relatively smoothly in Poland, due to the existence of non-communist elites and the exposure to the West much broader than in the case of other Soviet bloc countries. As a popular joke says, Poland was "the most cheerful barrack in the socialist camp". Moreover, the majority of former communist elites, nowadays called "post-communist", often "converted" from Marxism and espoused ideals of a liberal democracy, private market economy and strong links with the West.
- The early marketization phase brought market mechanism of price formation, convertibility of the currency, lifting of trade barriers and legal barriers of private entrepreneurship. As a response, over 2 million private companies emerged almost overnight and the picturesque show of "wild capitalism" began. Evidently, the proliferation of the private sector in "socialist Poland" helped a lot, especially since it was combined with the mindset composed of street smarts, natural entrepreneurship, risk proneness, and the culture of "cutting corners". Some of newly born private companies grew, some merged with others, some disappeared and left space for others, but until today, the sector of small and medium size enterprises provides for value added equal to 74.0% of Poland's GDP, exhibiting the gift of resistance to external shocks and employing 63.4% of the workforce (PARP 2018).
- The inflation control phase of transition was absolutely crucial for the further development of the economy plagued by hyperinflation (Balcerowicz 1995). Under the influence of "Chicago School" economists, hosting young Polish academics not such a long time ago who were hurriedly appointed as top new government officials, a brutal "shock therapy" was chosen as a remedy against Polish super-inflation. It consisted of such austerity measures as the elimination of subsidies aimed at supporting state owned enterprises or keeping prices of consumption items artificially low; tight credit control leading to a positive real interest rate; exchange rate devaluation at the new depreciated rate; administrative limitation of nominal wage growth; liberalization of all prices and the privatization of the formerly socialist economy. It was painful but it worked in

relatively short period of time. After the deep recession of 1990–1992, inflation was under control and economic growth resumed without interruption. Poland adopted the floating exchange rate regime, and became a financially viable business partner after successfully negotiating 50% foreign debt forgiveness.

- In Poland the market institutions building phase was propelled by a strong influence of the West, which was channeled through westernized elites and tightening economic ties to the global markets. Tax reform, banking system reform (including independent central bank and bank supervision) and the creation of capital markets opened to foreign investors played a key role. Institutional reforms produced a business environment friendly to foreign investors and spurred foreign direct investment in manufacturing, trade, services and financial institutions.
- Since the institutions building phase of transition produced results with a considerable delay, an antirecession economic policy was badly needed to appease massive dissatisfaction brought up by shock therapy and an 18% decline in GDP, massive unemployment, individual consumption decrease in numerous social groups while new fortunes arise etc. The tradition of militancy and a bitter political struggle enhanced an antirecession drive and postulates to abandon austerity policies. The "Strategy for Poland" initiated in 1994 by the then Minister of Finance Grzegorz Kołodko, embraced a pro-development approach to the fullest extent. It brought a 28% in GDP between 1994 and 1997, accompanied by a 30% reduction in unemployment and a 60% reduction of inflation (Kołodko 2000).
- The sustained growth policy appears to be last phase of successful transition. It is marked by a trade-off between an increase of current individual consumption and investment in the future, i.e. in technology, science, education, health, environment etc. This trade-off triggers a political strife and is steamed by it.

The above overview of transition phases, as applied to Poland, enables three conclusions to be drawn:

1. During the transition period, Poland leveraged its social, cultural and intellectual capital accumulated throughout modern history. Its uniqueness (as compared with other countries of the Soviet block) paid off handsomely.
2. The westernization of Polish elites enabled links with the western world. Both EU and the US provided financial assistance (massive private and public debt forgiveness) and expert advice, facilitating Poland's accession to such institutions as: the OECD, EBRD, IMF and finally paving the way for membership in the EU and NATO.
3. From the inside of the country, the transition was powered by emotions: hope, fear, growing aspirations. Emotions coupled with a real economic cycle and amplified by a democratic political cycle produced the consecutive phases of transition.

Similar mechanisms can be observed in much more detail, when the BDI complex coefficient is applied to Poland.

2 BDI Usefulness

We began our analysis of the Polish market economy in 1999. That year marked the tenth anniversary of the "Balcerowicz Plan", upon which this economy was built with very significant changes later introduced by Grzegorz Kołodko. The economic transformation into the mature free market was then complete. Thus, we can attempt to analyze the Polish economy according to the standards generally applied to "normal" developed market economies, without repeating the "uniqueness of transformation" mantra so popular in the economic analysis of Poland in the early 1990s. Nevertheless, some specific features of the Polish emerging market economy must be kept in mind, mainly the "normative GDP growth" standard, which amounts to at least 3% a year for the Polish economy. Even in spite of the clear symptoms of secular stagnation in the most developed countries of the world (Summers 2016a, b), the Polish economy must grow faster than the long range average for highly developed western economies. Fast growth is necessary in order to satisfy consumption appetites of the population generally comparing Polish and Western European (old EU) standards of living. With such a fast growth since 1999, Poland is successfully engaging itself in a "catching up" race with the old EU.

However, we should note that despite the dynamic changes 16 years is still a very modest statistical sequence. For example, Baker et al. (2015) analyze a period of 30 years, from 1985 to 2014. Of course, the period of 16 years can also be the subject of analysis, but the research and theoretical conclusions drawn from it must be viewed with due caution. In such a period, it is particularly difficult to identify particular business cycles, and it is even more difficult to present the mechanism of such cycles.

By studying the BDI dynamics and its relation to the changes in GDP, we may identify the classic short phases of the cycle, such as: depression, recovery, prosperity, and crisis, but not the long term periods of recession and growth, so popular in modern economic analyses. However, the short phases do not appear in regular cycles partially disturbing the functional balance, controllability and predictability of the system.

Our research on the Polish economy using the BDI as analytical instrument directs attention to a specific types of social expectations concerning the economy: *creational expectations*. Economic actors (households, enterprises, employees, consumers) expect that satisfactory prices of goods and labor (wages) will be created for them, but are not able to predict them and take them into account in their decisions. That's what optimism and assertiveness is all about. They expect their wishes to be fulfilled by others: government, markets, employers etc. Creational expectations hold a very high load of emotions, sometimes even aggression, often aroused and strengthened by the media. That directs us towards the "economy of emotions". Creational expectations may sometimes resemble the irrational expectations as defined by Akerloff and Schiller. While irrational expectations are decisively explanatory – they allow for an ex-post evaluation of phenomena – creational expectations are both explanatory and normative since they are often mixed with political activism and social media expressions in a way collectively "enforcing" certain solutions. In the 18 years under scrutiny (1999–2017), the BDI accurately explained and predicted changes in the economic policy of the state, in business and consumer strategies, and – above all – in Polish politics, by resorting to the analysis of social emotions and emotional expectations.

3 BDI Trends in 1999–2017

Poland is the only rational dependent economy in our sample, though close to the border line with emotionality. It is in a unique positioning, since – as our analysis shows – dependency is the most likely to be co-aligned with emotional nature of the economy. Such a unique position can be logically explained by history of Polish transition presented above. Poland is highly dependent upon the inflow of foreign capital in the form of FDI (foreign direct investment) responsible for large share of the total country's productive investment. FDI partly financed the government debt, while EU funds grossly contributed to financing critical infrastructure projects and supported agriculture. Export, mainly to the EU (Germany in particular), is considered as one of the most powerful growth engines. Poland also remains technologically dependent on its Western partners. Poland's "rationality" is justified by the painful experience of hyperinflation in the first years of transition. This painful experience facilitated imposing fiscal prudence and reasonable monetary policies. Also active participation of Poland in international structures and Formation of new elites played a positive role. However, the drift towards the group of emotional countries should be noted after 2015. It was powered by a spree of politically motivated unprecedented social expenditures.

The 45 available detailed components of the BDI, collapsed into its four middle-level indices, allow for the analysis of socio-economic development in 1999–2017 (Fig. 4.1), comparison with the GDP index (Fig. 4.2), and distinction of the business cycle phases in the Polish economy (Table 4.1).

Poland was the only European country which experienced consistent growth of the GDP during the entire period of analysis, including the world crisis time. It was considered a European "green island" from that point of view. However, changes in the BDI present quite a different, much more realistic picture. There were two drastic declines of the BDI in 2008, 2009 and 2012. The external economic functioning and social expectations were the most affected, while deterioration in the current social conditions remained at almost the same level during the entire 2008–2013 period. The application of our comprehensive middle-level index of internal economic conditions indicated a strong negative impact of the world crisis on the Polish domestic economy despite the consistent, albeit slightly slower, GDP growth.

Stabilization of the social conditions at the same level and the news about the world crisis have created pessimistic expectations for the future and a feeling of uncertainty, especially that this has happened in a condition of rapidly rising

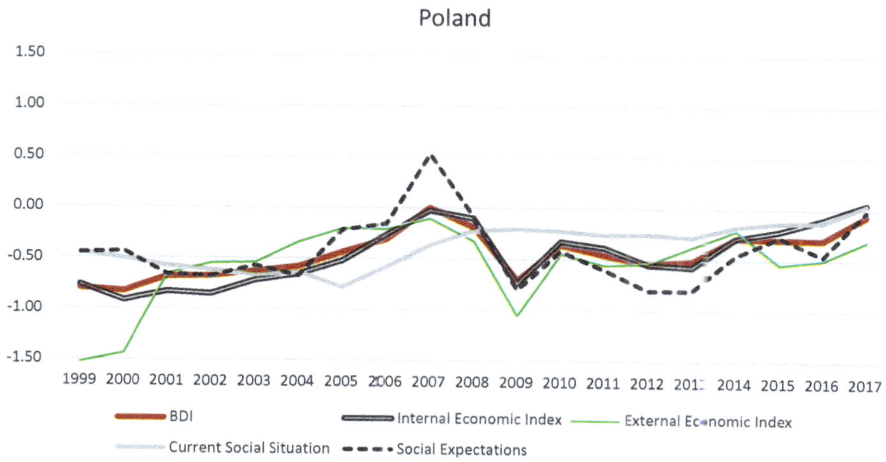

Fig. 4.1 Values of Poland's BDI and its four components in 1999–2017

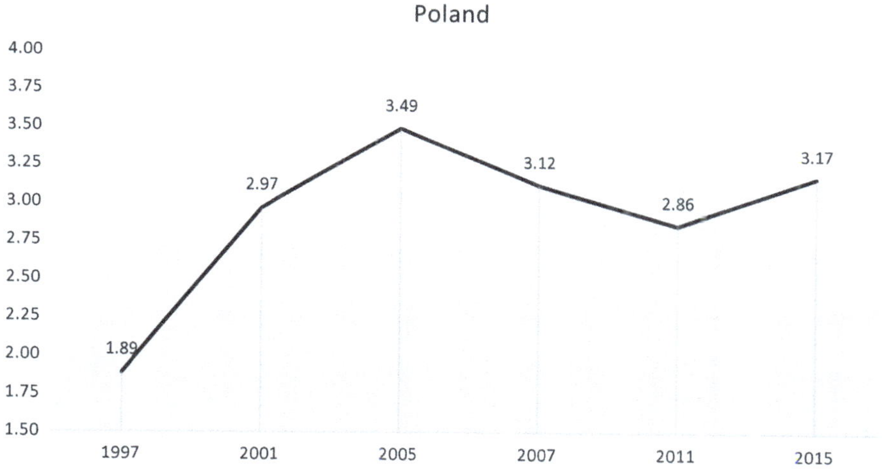

Fig. 4.2 Poland's political radicalism index

expectations influenced by a former good economic situation. All these factors resulted in the radicalization of the Polish political scene and a change of government in 2015.

The BDI and several other criteria help to distinguish several short periods in Poland's socio-economic development.

The meaning of the terms used in Table 4.1:

- (R): restrictive policy, Monetary Policy Council (MPC) decisions on the monetary policy to increase interest rates (R5 means five times in a row) and, on the fiscal policy, to reduce the public finance deficit;

Table 4.1 Phases of functional equilibrium and disequilibrium of the Polish economy from 1999 to 2017

	1999–2000	2000–2001	2001–2003	2003–2007	2007–2009	2009–2010	2010–2013	2013–2015	2016–2017
Balanced Development Index	Depression	Recovery	Depression	Prosperity	Crisis	Recovery	Depression	Recovery	Depression/ Prosperity
GDP	Normal growth	Normal growth	Abnormal growth	Above-normal growth	Normal growth	Abnormal growth	Abnormal growth	Normal growth	Abnormal growth
Investments	Abnormal growth	Crisis	Crisis	Above-normal growth	Crisis	Crisis	Recovery/ crisis	Normal growth	Crisis
Individual Consumption	Abnormal growth	Abnormal growth	Abnormal growth	Normal growth	Above-normal growth	Abnormal growth	Abnormal growth	Abnormal growth	Normal growth
European Market Conditions	Above-normal growth	Above-normal growth	Normal growth	Above-normal growth	Crisis	Abnormal growth	Abnormal growth	Normal growth	Normal growth
Central European Market Conditions	Abnormal growth	Abnormal growth	Abnormal growth	Above-normal growth	Crisis	Abnormal growth	Abnormal growth	Abnormal growth	Normal growth
Fiscal Policy	R	E	E	E/R	R/E	E	E	E	E
Monetary Policy	R (5)	R (2)/E (7)	E (21)	E (8)/R (1)/E (7)/R (4)	R (8)/E (6)	E (4)	R (5)/E (8)	E (8)	E
Expected Return on Investment and Consumption	Growth	Decline	-No changes	Strong growth	Strong decline	Growth	No changes/ decline	Weak growth	Decline
Media Narration and Political Changes	Weaken growth	Weaken growth	Support growth	Strongly weaken growth	Strongly support growth	Support growth	Weaken growth	Strongly weaken growth	Strongly weaken growth

Social Predictions	Moderate optimism growth	Moderate optimism growth	Moderate pessimism growth	Significant optimism growth	Significant pessimism growth	Significant optimism growth	Significant pessimism growth	Significant pessimism growth	Significant optimism growth
Social Assessments of the Current Situation	Significant decline	Slight decline	Fluctuations	Significant improvement	Fluctuations	Significant improvement	Significant decline	Slight decline	Significant improvement
(Objective) Social Situation	Significant decline	Significant decline	Fluctuations	Significant improvement	Fluctuations (beginning of a decline)	Slight improvement	Significant decline	Slight decline	Significant improvement
Hierarchy of Regulators Restoring Functional Equilibrium	Markets Firms State Households	Markets State Households Firms	State Markets Households Firms	Firms Households Markets State	Markets State Firms Households	State Markets Households Firms	State Markets Households Firms	Markets Firms State Households	Households Firms Markets State

- (E): expansionary policy, MPC decisions on the monetary policy to cut interest rates (E7 means seven times in a row) and, on the fiscal policy, to increase the public finance deficit;
- Normal growth: growth of 3–4.5% of GDP, investment, and individual consumption;
- Above-normal growth: growth above 4.5% of GDP, investment, and individual consumption;
- Abnormal growth: growth below 3% of GDP, investment, and individual consumption;
- Depression: the state of the economy and society characterized by a lack of growth of the general or partial BDI;
- Crisis: the state of the economy and society characterized by a decrease in the general or partial BDI;
- Prosperity: the state of the economy and society characterized by a strong increase in the general or partial BDI;
- Recovery: the state of the economy and society characterized by a weak growth (0–1.0 of the scale….) of the general or partial BDI;
- The assessment of the impact of the media narrative and policy changes that weaken, encourage, or support growth: conclusions of descriptive case studies and time periods

4 Characteristics of the Analyzed Periods

1999–2000 GDP growth was accompanied by a slight decrease in the general BDI index of socio-economic development as well as equally slight decline in middle-level indices of external and internal economic conditions. However, social expectations were moderately (one can say negligibly) improving during this period.

In the face of the then prevailing conditions, events, actions, as well as development in the previous period, the 1999 growth of GDP by 4.1% can be described as bordering on recession. It became apparent that – after 5.2% growth in 1994, 7.0% in 1995, 6.1% in 1996, 6.9% in 1997, and 4.8% in 1998 – the economy started to slow down significantly, though the GDP was still growing. The conservative-liberal coalition AWS-UW (Solidarity Electoral Alliance – Freedom Union), in power since late 1997, was preparing its own "engines" of economic growth for the following years, showing no interest in the "engines" inherited from the liberal-left ("post-communist") SLD-PSL (Democratic Left Alliance – Polish People's Party) coalition. Among others, the reason for this was the readout of the current account balance, which in 1999 reached a dangerous record-breaking level of –7.5%.

Restrictive fiscal and monetary policies and the intensive "cooling" of economy, introduced in attempt to improve this balance, led to a slowdown in the GDP growth. This had a negative impact on household as well as business spending, and resulted in worsening current social conditions and – in the next period – social expectations. The political situation and prevailing narration in the media contributed to a very slow improvement in the social expectations in this period and their deterioration later on. Social expectations and the functional balance could have been only be improved through political changes. The AWS-UW coalition collapsed in 2000 and the Democratic Left Alliance (SLD) received an overwhelming advantage in the polls with a clear view of taking power in 2001.

- The second wave of very wide privatization;

The significant in 1999, the second year of the AWS-UW coalition, the pace of implementation of the "four reforms" accelerated. The coalition reformed education, the pension system, regional administration and health care. Unia Wolności (Freedom Union) and Leszek Balcerowicz pushed for new growth engine concepts, such as:

- Reductions in personal and corporate taxes which was even the IMF considered as too liberal and distorting to the competition for capital in the world;
- A relatively uniform VAT rate for the entire economy, but retaining the preferential 3% for the agriculture;
- Preparations for Poland's accession to the European Union on the fastest track possible;
- Transition to a floating exchange rate of the Polish zloty to world currencies.

The four reforms were to significantly contribute to further socio-economic development. This is particularly true of the launch of the Open Pension Funds in 1999, instigated by the hope that they will mobilize private investment and contribute to development of the Polish capital market. The administrative reform was supposed to contribute to the greater rationality of public expenditures and their pro-development nature, as was the establishment of the Health Insurance Funds. The educational reform was to ensure more favorable conditions for young people to enter the labor market. The increase in private investments was to be further stimulated by extensive privatization. Privatization revenues increased from PLN 7.1 billion in 1998 to PLN 13.4 billion in 1999 and to the record high of PLN 27 billion in 2000. The increase in privatization revenues allowed to attract foreign capital – USD 6.4 billion in 1999, compared to USD 5 billion in 1998 and a mere USD 3 billion in 1997 – and mitigate the danger of a high negative current account balance. A major reduction in taxes was viewed as pro-development. However, the tax reform was vetoed by President Aleksander Kwaśniewski under pressure from the Democratic Left Alliance (SLD), which was gaining increasing electoral support. A triple political scene began to crystallize: the AWS-UW coalition gradually splintered into the neo-liberals and the neo-conservatists, while the Democratic Left Alliance and the presidential camp began to assume a neo-socialist orientation.

All in all, the very short first period of our analysis already indicated a discrepancy between a positive picture of Polish development as measured by the GDP and a negative one as measured by the BDI or by three out of four of its middle-level indices. In the BDI terms, this was a period of slight depression, while it is considered a growth period in the GDP terms. These differences will become even more apparent in the next period. This shows the advantages of the BDI analysis as orange or red light warning against the crisis.

2000–2001 This was a period of a short recovery according to both the BDI and GDP. While GDP growth wasn't very impressive, both external and internal conditions of the economy, as measured by our middle-level indices, remarkably improved, the former even quite spectacularly. However, social warnings of a possible future recession were increasing during this period: both social expectations and current social conditions were deteriorating. Thus, BDI growth was achieved mostly because of a very substantial improvement in the economy, not translated into a similar improvement in social conditions. Growth in GDP, individual consumption and investment were moderate, despite being strongly driven by a significant improvement in the external economic functioning. This was due to the increase in the importance of such factors as:

- A successful long-term policy of reducing the current account deficit to GDP ratio;
- Increased confidence in the Polish economy;
- Strong capital inflows, associated with the increase in confidence, a comprehensive privatization program and a strengthening of the Polish zloty in relation to the Euro.

Deteriorating social indicators, especially expectations, heralded the crisis due to the fact that the reduction of the budget deficit required a decline in social and individual consumption. The functional balance, understood as opposite to the discrepancy between developmental domains, increased in this period, perhaps too much to ensure development in the near future. That required a policy which would knock the economy from being close to equilibrium into the developmental process.

June 2000 saw the effective and formal collapse of the AWS-UW coalition, in power since the fall of 1997. Until the elections in September 2001, both parties supported each other mainly to retain power. In the first half of 2000, Leszek Balcerowicz, the Minister of Finance pushed to reduce the budget deficit by 2003 as a realistic and necessary plan. The plan was supposed to allow Poland to join the European Union quickly and, from January 2003, to "stop the engine" that created the dangerously high deficit in the balance of payments, reduce the still high inflation, stimulate private investment, and even allow the early adoption of the euro. By mid-year, the idea collapsed entirely because the government began to favor social packages. Their launch ended in 2001, with the disclosure of the deficit first reaching PLN 60 billion and later even PLN 90 billion. As a result, Leszek Balcerowicz decided, as the then President of Bank of Poland, to implement the remainder of the liberal program which he attained at the end of 2000. The Polish National Bank and the Monetary Policy Council conducted a restrictive monetary policy throughout 2000, doubling the interest rates. On February 24, they raised the reference rate from 16.5% to 17.5%, and on August 31 to 19.0%. Despite this, the inflation rate was still quite high and the current account balance of payments was still highly precarious. This situation strongly limited the government and the central bank's ability to stimulate the economy with a policy mix in the next year, when the global economy significantly slowed down. Therefore, the Polish government and central bank were not prepared for the upcoming global economic slowdown in 2001.

However, as for the BDI level, the key issue seemed to be the volume of growth in household consumption. It amounted only to 2.8% and decreased to 2.1% in the following year. The decline repeated two more times during the period covered by our study and always directly related to profound political changes (change of governments). In 2001, the government changed from AWS-UW to SLD-PSL.

2001–2003 was a period of slow-down or stabilization with almost negligible improvement in 2003. While the external economic conditions were still improving, though at a much slower pace than before, the BDI and its three remaining middle-level components stayed at an almost stable level. The middle-level index of the external (international) functioning of the Polish economy continued to improve despite the decrease in both foreign and domestic investments.

The economy was desperately defended by an expansionary fiscal and monetary policy (21 interest rate cuts). Low domestic and foreign savings – which could not have been stimulated by a monetary policy and by the expected return on investment – was associated with a week increase in consumption. The attempt of Grzegorz Kołodko, Minister of Finance and Deputy Prime Minister at the time, to reform public finances encountered strong social resistance. However, even in a reduced form, it resulted in a "normative growth" of Poland's GDP, namely (3%) in the final year of this period.

2003–2007 was a longer period of pre-crisis socioeconomic development. Apart from small fluctuations, both the GDP and the BDI and all its four main components showed a clear upward trend. This was instigated by good international economic conditions in the previous period. These international conditions started to rise again quite rapidly. All in all, it was a period of prosperity and hope, characterized by overall improvement. While this improvement was apparent in all four domains of socio-economic development, it was exceptional, especially in the formerly stable social expectations and in the external and internal economic conditions. The middle-level index of current social conditions, though improving, was at a relatively much lower level than both economic indices, which could have been the main reason of the relatively mild effect exerted in Poland by the world financial crisis.

In an improved external economic environment, GDP growth accelerated. Individual consumption growth almost kept pace with the GDP, although it grew at a somewhat slower rate. After a short-term slowdown at the end of the previous period, the improvement in the external aspects of economic functioning accelerated again. The internal economic condition and the social situation also improved, albeit with a 1-year delay. This resulted in an unprecedented increase in social optimism and expectations for the future. This large increase in optimism that started from the acceleration led to an imbalanced development, marked by a progressive increase in the standard deviation of the BDI's four components. While both the external (international) and internal aspects of economic performance improved, the increase of inconsistency stemmed from excessive social optimism and fast improvement in the current economic conditions.

The monetary policy at that time was pragmatic: it was a mixture of expansionary and restrictive measures. Although the BDI grew faster than the GDP, the progressive reduction in the balance between the four composite index components led to a gradual loss of controllability of the system and posed a danger of reversing the development trend.

This positive phase of the business cycle in Poland and the world in 2003–2007 was the longest in the entire period under analysis. However, the analysis of changes in four socio-economic domains measured by the middle-level suggested potential risks that did materialize after 2007.

As in the past, external economic factors drove the entire development mechanism during this period. The GDP grew very rapidly in European countries and quite rapidly in the US. Asia did well, and even Africa started to make a positive impact on the world thanks to the emerging attractiveness for investors. However, the artificiality of economic growth in the world (above all in the US) was driven by the extremely expansive monetary policy of A. Greenspan at the helm of US Federal Reserve, who reduced interest rates to 1%, and also by the irresponsible policy – under George W. Bush's administration – of stimulating the economy by financing housing construction with subprime loans. The securitization of these loans in the form of such vehicles as Collateralized Debt Obligation or Assets Backed Security contributed greatly to the fragility of the American financial system. Had it not been for the US' policies, the world economy would have entered a crisis already in 2003–2004 nevertheless, but probably much milder than the one that began in 2007, which – as some economists believe – has continued to this very day. During the hypothetical earlier crisis, the global economy would have probably more easily responded to solutions aimed at healthy economic growth. Despite the highly negative phenomena at its source, the international economic situation also created favorable conditions for development in Poland, as indicated by the exceptionally good index of external economic conditions of the Polish economy. Many factors that influenced the development of the BDI in this period assumed very positive values: external factors, internal factors, domestic and foreign savings, assessment of the current situation by the society, expectations for the future, fiscal policy, monetary policy, and even the expected profitability of investments and consumption, which grew dynamically. However, during this period, three elements heralded the danger of crisis: the ratio of real-to-potential GDP, media narration accompanying political changes, and – above all – the level of functional imbalance.

In this artificially positive period, the Polish economy paid for strong GDP growth and even stronger BDI growth (*sic!*) by losing a functional balance between its four domains. In 2007, strong limitations of development, paid in this manner, became apparent in such bottlenecks as excessive wage growth limiting the profitability of investments and shifting savings to consumption, declining power plant capacity and efficiency, insufficient infrastructure, especially transport and road infrastructure, and an increasingly negative current balance of payments. A severely deteriorating functional balance between not only four developmental domains but also the abovementioned detailed economic features made for an negative media narrative and political change. This created a fairly convenient basis for the takeover of power by PiS-Samoobrona-LPR (Law and Justice– Self-defense – League of Polish Families) coalition in 2005 and the presidency of Lech Kaczyński.

Despite these dangers, Poland's generally favorable economic and social situation – both objective and subjective – created missed opportunities for reform expected by the society. The failure to take advantage of these opportunities contributed to the later reversal of the trend and another change of government.

2007–2009 marked a beginning of world financial crisis and political change in Poland. Nevertheless, Poland managed to maintain positive economic growth measured by GDP and the level of consumption. However, the overall situation was unstable and uncertain. The years of the global financial crisis were characterized by a significant decline in the functioning of the Polish economy in the external (international) environment and a very drastic decline of social expectations. As mentioned above, Poland was nonetheless one of the exceptions on a global scale due to continued – albeit slower – GDP growth. This did not prevent a sharp decline of the more comprehensively measured internal economic situation. The increase in GDP did not translate into an improvement in the social situation. While it did not deteriorate, it did not improve either, despite very high expectations at the beginning of this period. The growth of income and individual consumption stalled, as did social expenditure. The collapse of the PIS-Samoobrona-LPR coalition gave rise to high support for the new government. However, this support dropped very quickly after a brief period of "honeymoon" similar to the one, which occurred after the previous change of government. However, this time the decline in support was accompanied by a sharp decline in the previously very optimistic expectations. This resulted from a combination of a noticeable decline in external and internal economic conditions and unchanging (only negligibly deteriorating) current social conditions. Emerging social pessimism was coincident with the declarations of politicians and economists proclaiming the need for further budgetary savings and a with conviction that the crisis will also reach Poland, even if in a milder form.

The impending highly dangerous financial and economic world crisis led to the adoption of emergency measures. However, Poland's GDP dampened this shocking impact and Poland went down in history as a "green island" with relatively good economic growth. Other European countries and the US had a clearly negative growth rate at that time, while 2008–2009 saw the average GDP growth rate in Poland at +3.3%. The consistently rising GDP provided an unrealistically optimistic picture of Poland during the crisis in the eyes of politicians and economists (not in public opinion), while the BDI better depicted real effects of this crisis. This has had significant economic and political consequences even to this day. The overall situation is strongly influenced by social factors, the media narrative, and political life next to economic policy changes, which weaken the positive impact of GDP growth for the society.

The most significant conclusion from the crisis period analysis is the fact that the use of GDP growth alone as an indicator of development results in a picture, which suggests that Poland avoided the global financial crisis. At the same time, the BDI analysis reveals the negative impact of the crisis on socio-economic development. The BDI accounts equally for economic and social aspects and characterizes interrelated external and internal aspects of the economic situation more comprehensively than GDP, so it is a better measure, especially in turbulent times.

2009–2010 was a period that we may characterize as the end of social and economic depression, reassuming development, and a rise in hope caused by the "green island syndrome". Poland went through the crisis relatively unscathed, although it did leave its mark of a wider social and economic dimension. The European economic situation was improving, and we could see a revival in the Polish economy. The monetary and financial policy of the government became more expansive. The current social situation did not deteriorate a lot during the crisis and remained at a similar level. All the remaining aspects of development improved, especially social expectations. The overall BDI increased along with the growing equilibrium of its components. This meant the danger of a renewed slowdown in social and economic development. On the other hand, one can assume that a higher level of functional balance resulted in the better controllability of the system, which created another missed opportunity for necessary reforms.

All these constitute another argument for the particular role of social factors in the development of a functional balance in Poland and the specificity of Polish economic and political transformations in general. From the viewpoint of purely economic factors, this phase should have ended in 2011, when GDP growth was still relatively high (4.8% as compared to the 3.7% growth in 2010). At the end of 2010, the BDI started to significantly decline, a year earlier than the significant slowdown (though not decline) in GDP growth. However, in 2009–2010, both economic and social factors were on the positive side. There was a significant increase in social predictions, fiscal and monetary policy was expansionary, internal economic factors were positive, which positively influenced the BDI even with the presence of negative external factors. However, the balance between four developmental domains increased to a very high level. This has created a danger for further development.

2010–2013 was a period of renewed socioeconomic decline. Pessimism rose sharply due to failed hopes raised in the previous period, in parallel with the increase in pessimism about the future. Even relatively stable social condition slightly deteriorated. The external and internal conditions of the economy deteriorated much more. GDP and consumption growth slowed down, despite still positive dynamics compared with the rest of Europe. The mixed monetary policy contained both restrictive and expansive elements. There was a clear decline in social expectations for the future but current social conditions remained almost unchanged.

This raises the key theoretical and practical question: where does the descriptive and predictive capacity of the BDI come from? Obviously, explanations must be sought in relationships between components of the BDI. The difference between GDP and the BDI comes mostly from the changes in external economic factors and in social expectations but also from current social conditions. Thus, the key role is played here by social factors, including subjective and emotional factors created by the media narrative; which may stir the need for political change. The response to these factors was an unstable economic policy: the government hesitated between restrictive and expansionary financial policies and announced desperate programs of the partial liquidation of open retirement funds. There was no coherent economic strategy. The Polish National Bank initially raised interest rates five times and then lowered them eight times. At the end of 2013, however, there is a slow improvement and we are entering the recovery period – 2013–2015.

2013–2015 2013 is usually considered as a year ending the in the world crisis, although this is a rather arbitrary date. The improvement was achieved "artificially" through massive programs of Quantitative Easing (or in other words printing money). In spite of the fact that this was not practiced in Poland Polish GDP was again rising above the necessary "normal" 3%. Its distance to Germany and other "old EU countries" was significantly reduced. This was achieved thanks to the very good co-production of the regulators of the economy: markets, enterprises and the state, unfortunately with the weakening of the households regulator (A. Noga 2016). The weakness of traditional economic indicators of economic conditions, with GDP at the forefront, was also the most visible during this period. The good economic situation and good functioning of markets, companies and the state do not ensure the functional equilibrium of the system. The curve of the internal economic situation has been growing strongly since 2013. The GDP is on a very good growth path, reaching 4.6% in the last quarter of 2015, despite the worsening of the external situation. Its supply capabilities, without Keynesian support, give it a chance to rise above 5% in 2016–2019. Both the lack of GDP decline in Poland in 2009, as in many countries around the world, as well as entering the path of high GDP growth, show that the 25 years of transformation of the Polish economy have brought definite successes. Successes in the economic and technological sphere, but not in the socio-political sphere.

The disenchantment of the large, poorer part of society was growing. It surfaced with powerful dissatisfaction caused by the necessary reforms of the pension system and the rising retirement age. Reforms were carried out too late, without convincing public opinion and offering some sort of compensation. Therefore, despite the good economic situation, the social assessments of the current situation did not increase, and in 2015, heated by media narration, social expectations dropped sharply. The deteriorating public opinion mood was heavily politically exploited by the far right PiS party, which won the presidency and the parliamentary majority, obtaining 37% of popular support.

2016–2017 To what extent can the BDI help us understand the end of last phase in 2015 and the start of a new one in 2016? The analysis of the BDI mechanism in previous periods clearly shows that the 2013–2015 socio-economic phase could not last any longer. Firstly, due to two groups of social factors: social expectations clearly dropped at the turn of 2015–2016, and the current assessment of the social situation did not increase. This happened with the strongly accelerated economy, which even recorded an impressive EUR 50 billion in exports to Germany. GDP growth fell to less than 3% in 2016 instead of the expected 5% or more.

It seems that the present PiS government fell into a trap of inevitable decline, which the party itself prophesized in the election rhetoric without real belief. Our model indicates the possibility of a crisis or a significant depression. According to this analysis, 2016 might have been already be the year of depression. This year saw a drop in investment; a key development factor. Such a "cave-in" could not be an isolated incident.

Avoiding the potential depression trap of 2016–2017 was made possible because of the intensive direct financing of households in the form of so-called 500+ program, i.e. a social allowance for every second and next child in the family. The cost of this program at the beginning of 2017 was approaching 1% GDP, and in the perspective of 2019, the year of parliamentary elections, it may reach even 2.5% of GDP, especially when supplemented by other social subsidies. All these measures were aimed at building up political support and providing fuel for roaring consumption engine of growth. In 2016–2017, the previous necessary reforms of the pension system and the labor markets were withdrawn, considerably improving the assessment of current social conditions by the population and expectations for the future. The only question is how long can the budget sustain such a positive business climate without triggering the wave of inflation and a considerable increase of investment share in the GDP.

In our analysis, the period 2016–2017 was therefore a very strange period. In the synthetic table presented above, we have defined this period as: depression / prosperity. Due to socio-political factors, instead of a possible increase in GDP above 5%, the Polish economy achieved growth below 3% in 2016. That was below the "norm" necessary to close the distance to Western European countries. A strong, populist, Keynesian type social policy has allowed the economy to return to growth above 5% in 2017, but this is a different path from the rational supply path that has been emerging since 2015, with growing rather than receding investments. With this supply path maintained and the inclusion of Keynesian-demand social stimulation in 2017, GDP growth should be over 7%, as in the following years (e.g. 2018, 2019). All in all, the huge role of social and political factors has changed the business cycle in Poland, which is shown by the BDI, not the GDP.

5 Lessons from the BDI Analysis for Poland

Creative expectations have both an explanatory and normative value. On the one hand they enable us to explain the changes of socio-economic climate, from the other they enforce certain solutions (for example more spending on social welfare) through political mechanisms.

In spite of all the successes of socio-economic development in Poland and unquestionable rationality of public choices observed throughout the years covered by our analysis (1999–2017), the grains of possible future failure originate from the increasingly excessive influence of short-sighted (electoral cycle driven) politics on economic life. Poland seems to be moving slowly towards the category of emotional countries, such as Greece, with all the related dangers incoming. In the situation of low and decreasing private investments, excessive social spending covered by public debt financed by international borrowers make the country excessively vulnerable to inevitable external shocks (such as the crisis in the euro zone) flattening the productivity curve and a GDP growth slow down. Clear signals are already in sight: in 2018 private investment reached a historical low of 13.5% (Rzeczpospolita daily June 19–20, 2019).

The observed phases of the business cycle are short. The picture spells out volatility because of the emotional nature of creative expectations. People hope for a better future and do not want to wait too long. A quick return on investments is expected and aspirations grow higher and higher in a country fully exposed to the "old EU" and its standards. When disappointed, people become restless and the ground for political change is ready. In such a way, the emotional dimension of the business cycle becomes the source of positive development at the same the time, and contains the grains of potential failure. People's hopes and positive expectations push up consumers' and investors' confidence and spur entrepreneurial initiatives. Disappointment and fear (more likely when expectations are high) have the opposite effects and bring about political instability. The volatility of the cycle can make it almost hysterical. Poland as a post-transition economy and relatively young (perhaps not fully entrenched) democracy seems particularly vulnerable to such hysterical changes of a socio-economic climate.

The upper phase of the business cycle and strong GDP growth do not guarantee the reelection of a ruling political party or coalition (examples: 2007, 2015). Emotions prevail driven by the fulfillment of aspirations, feelings of justice, dignity, envy etc.

Poland provides an example of high volatility of the system coexisting with high degree of inertia of institutions, organizational cultures and even policies. Impatience is constantly confronted with immobility or a slow pace of change. In order to gain support and appease expectations bitterly divided politicians increase social spending instead of embarking on the thorny road of structural and institutional reforms of the German type conditioned by broad political support.

We gathered our conclusions about the economics of emotions in Poland: 1999–2017 in the following 13 detailed findings on the development of the BDI and its components:

1. Anticipating (dynamizing) elements that trigger subsequent phases of the cycle include external economic conditions (dependency syndrome) and social expectations (hopes, fears, anxieties, obsessions), concerning the entire economy rather than the personal situation.
2. Both the internal economic situation and the current standard of living, but also satisfaction with one's own and the family's situation, are passive (secondary) in most periods, which means that they agree with the replacement of leading elements. They can occur both alternately and simultaneously.
3. The mutual interaction of the above four groups of factors effects the overall BDI, which measures social and economic development – as opposed to GDP

that only measures economic growth – and also allows us to assess the level of functional balance; hence, the controllability of the system.

4. The higher the standard deviations of individual sub-indices (mid-level indices that measure the level of each of the four groups of indicators), the lower the level of the functional balance. In other words, the greater the "volatility" and internal "mismatch" of the system components, the lower the balance.
5. The disturbance in balance – that is, the increase in the standard deviation – results in a direction shift of the economic and social development trend as measured by the BDI. This change may be both positive (increase) and negative (decrease) for socioeconomic development.
6. Measured by the BDI, socioeconomic development has several objective external correlates which may be treated either as an indicator of the ultimate goal of development (human flourishing) or as a confirmation of the index's relevance as an indicator of socioeconomic development. These correlates are the personal well-being index, life satisfaction, inverted suicide rate, and the level of support for political opposition (especially anti-system opposition). The level of balance measures the controllability of the system.
7. The high level of balance means low standard deviation and low variation in the pace of change of individual indicators that form the overall BDI. This means a stagnation. In order to make the system more dynamic, the system needs to be spurred by reforms. The problem lies in finding the extent of the imbalance that will not affect the controllability of the system negatively. Each major change calls for a specific "counterweight". In other words, change in each of the four dimensions of socio-economic balance requires adjustments in other dimensions. For example improved internal economic situation, requires improvement in current social conditions. Such principle of rational policies have been followed to great extend in the time covered by our BDI analysis.
8. One of the parameters of the internal economic situation – individual consumption – is of particular importance in influencing both the satisfaction with the present situation and future expectations. It is a kind of intermediary variable that amplifies the influence of other factors. Thus, when the general (internal) economic situation deteriorates, the decline in individual consumption intensifies dissatisfaction and pessimism. However, when there is no decline in consumption (or, rather, its growth rate so far) dissatisfaction with the worsening situation is reduced (or "suspended"). In the same way, the increase in consumption "beyond one's means" increases satisfaction and optimism.
9. A good economic situation and the high level of satisfaction with one's own situation and the family's do not guarantee a high level of stability (functional balance) if they co-occur with anxiety and uncertainty about the future of the country, workplace, and family. Conversely, optimistic expectations neutralize the negative effects of dissatisfaction with a worse economic situation.
10. All dependencies between the four dimensions of balance (the external and internal economic situation, current social situation and expectations, the mood) are immersed in the "grey area" of media influence – including, perhaps

most importantly, social media – and political rhetoric that comes from various sources. Facts, events, and even personal feelings and moods are subject to constant redefinition and reinterpretation. However, in this information chaos, leading narratives such as "green island" or "Poland in ruins," surface but only periodically and usually for a short amount of time. These are loosely rooted in reality. This relationship is defined by informational methods, which often use emotions. This may explain a certain "hyperactivity" or "hysteria" of the public opinion when it strongly reacts to various rumors, distorted information, or slogans, but also to truly individual and collective events and experiences.

11. Expectations expressed in this way encourage the ruling party and the opposition to formulate reform ideas and programs in the hope that they will help them to gain or maintain public support. However, as a rule, their programs take shape only after numerous modifications and in a more or less truncated and altered form. This is the result of social resistance against change, political struggles, and conflicts of interests; especially the resistance of bureaucracy against inconvenient solutions. As a result, the system is subjected to "tremors," which are expressed in greater standard deviations of our indices.
12. In the short term, this leads to a reduction in the level of functional balance, but in the longer term (about 3 years), it brings more optimistic expectations that increase resilience ("anti-fragility") to the possible decline in objective parameters. In other words, there is room for further reforms. The window of opportunity for reforms opens during the time of dissatisfaction and anxiety and can be broadened when reforms bring initial positive results and anxiety gives way to hope.
13. The entire abovementioned business cycle mechanism is stochastic: we may ascribe every relationship with a probability – more or less accurately – which overlaps with other relationships of a similar nature. Both the time and actions of system and non-system actors, but also of external factors like the international economic situation, are difficult to predict and trigger further consequences. This is due to the high intensity of emotions and the cognitive, competence, and motivational limitations of the collective and individual actors involved in the complex process of shaping the socioeconomic and political situation.

A nut shell conclusion from the in-depth case study of Poland is simple. The BDI is not only more complex than other indices of socio-economic well-being but also indicates the level of socio-economic balance. The level of balance denotes the phases of the business cycle in the most complex way and indicates chances of policy shifts. The BDI analysis can be used to predict changes of the socio-economic climate and to design policies. Human emotions, subjective assessments of the current situation and expectations for the future play a key role in modifying "hard" economic variables. The economy becomes social and political, in consequence unpredictable on the grounds of a purely economic analysis. An interdisciplinary approach embodied by the BDI is needed.

The concept of creational expectations and the economics of emotions, developed in our analyses of the Polish economy – seems potentially applicable to many other countries, including the United Kingdom after the Brexit referendum and the United States of America after the victory of Donald Trump in the presidential election. Summers (2016b) mentions this matter, although he refers to the concept of macroeconomic populism presented by Dornbusch and Edwards (1989), based on their research of Latin American countries in the 1970s. However, the concept of macroeconomic populism does not include systematic studies of the dynamics of changes in relations between social and economic factors – as does the BDI – but is limited to a general ("macroeconomic") descriptive and hypothetical dependence of economic policy on unrealistic social expectations.

Chapter 5
BDI: The New Kid in the Toolbox of Political Economy

1 Prediction Value of the BDI Analysis

The BDI may prove increasingly useful for the analysis of business cycles. How does it account for the brevity of the subsequent phases of the business cycle and allows us to forecast future crises? This is done through incorporating the measurement of public expectations and social assessments of the current situation into the BDI. The economy is not so much marked by transitions from one phase of the cycle to another, but by functional balance disruptions. The system is characterized by a high degree of inertia that can be shaken off by social aspirations and political games. Their effects, both positive and negative, appear with a considerable delay, oftentimes long after the departure of politicians whose decisions have shaped the system's balance.

In the economics of emotions, public expectations tend to be described in terms of: optimism, pessimism, anxiety, uncertainty, rather than defined as rational, irrational, extrapolative or adaptive. Emotions are accompanied by hope that acts as a driving force. They often morph into creative expectations: someone will brush away our anxiety and uncertainty, someone will transform pessimism into optimism. Society expects it, however, within a fairly short period, a maximum of 2–3 years. In vain… and then the new emotions of disillusionment start a new cycle. The BDI index helps to forecast such short cycles because it contains the emotional side of the economy in active interplay with hard economic factors.

Also, a number of factors contribute to the shortening of contemporary business cycles. The following should be noted:

- Politicians at all levels operate in short political cycles (up to 2–3 years), which is strongly related to public expectations and other factors, and is often reflected

A. K. Koźmiński et al., *The Balanced Development Index for Europe's OECD Countries, 1999–2017*, SpringerBriefs in Economics,
https://doi.org/10.1007/978-3-030-39240-6_5

in a rigorous negative selection among members of the political class, because short cycles and emotional volatility preclude professional and rational policy making;
- Public sector managers, appointed by politicians, are forced to follow "short termism" and shortening business cycles in the private sector. In the search for instant solutions, public expectations are met with symbolic measures amplified by propaganda and PR actions covering all kind of media (including social). That's why public services reforms in such sectors as: education, health care, energy or environment protection are so difficult, so costly and mostly missing the point. Such a situation builds up the "hit and run" mind set among public sector managers. Public opinion cannot turn a blind eye to that, and as a consequence, becomes even more emotional and volatile;
- The shortening of business cycles in the private sector is due to high speed competition and high speed management practices. Globalization imposes "competing in a flat world". Life cycles of products and technologies tend to shorten as well. Management compensation systems are co-aligned with short time horizons of business concepts replacing old fashioned long term strategies;
- Shareholders expect a quick and high return on their investment. Otherwise they start looking for alternative investment opportunities. Such moves are accelerated by the free worldwide flow of capital, professional advisory services and globalized investment banking. Capital is abundant, but "patient money" is hard to find. This is particularly true in the "emerging markets", where investors follow the "high risk high yield" principle and hurriedly withdraw their money when perceived risk is on the rise;

The economics of emotions allow us, therefore, to take into consideration a number of factors that contribute to the shortening of business cycle phases. It seems that the BDI analysis can help to explain the dynamics of transition to subsequent phases of the cycle and between the state of equilibrium and functional imbalance. In other words – what makes the cycle turn phases so quickly? In the periods of recovery and boom creative expectations are on the rise as well. They can stimulate either structural reforms aimed at sustainable socio-economic development in the long term, or further stimulate consumption growth at the cost of a decrease of investment and deficit state spending. From the political point of view, the reforms path is more risky because reforms usually bring a temporary worsening of the situation of certain groups of the population (like the temporary work force in Spain). The public assessment of the current situation and expectations for the future may deteriorate, bringing about fertile grounds for political change. Further consumption expansion carries the same type of risk in the longer perspective. The risk is bigger, however, because reckless consumption increase puts the financial stability of the country and, by consequence, the economic foundations of further development into jeopardy. Venezuela provides an extreme example of such a consumption driven slide below the subsistence level.

The changes in location of particular countries on rational-emotional and independent-dependent dimensions provides information necessary to assess the importance of these dimensions in the dynamics of socio-economic development. A good example would be looking at the location of countries in three different years: 2011 and 2014, i.e. the years of recovery from two previous crisis times, and 2017, i.e. the last year of our analysis and a year of continuous socio-economic development.

The first conclusion that comes out of a crisis in countries that were emotional but supposedly is that they are actually strongly dependent on the international economic environment. This was the price paid, among others, for previous economic behavior not compatible with the international strength of the economy. Italy, Portugal and Spain clearly belong to this group. These are countries of volatile economies which suffered the most during the crisis mostly due to excessive spending resulting from high aspirations. They are still emotional, a feature confirmed by more recent social turbulence, but assumed their position as being highly dependent on international influences. Slovakia has to be added to these countries if the criterion of .50 correlation is very strictly applied, but it remains located on the border line in all 3 years. The movement of Ireland from dependent rational to dependent emotional group is more interesting and untypical. Overcoming the crisis in this relatively well functioning country was followed by a greater influence of social expectations on economic functioning.

On the other extreme, the group of independent rational countries is the most stable. Its composition did not change with only one exception, namely Denmark advancing to this group from the independent emotional one. The group embraces the most mature, strong and developed European economies, which did not have to pay the price of higher dependency for overcoming the crisis.

Thus, the most movement between different categories of the socio-economic systems were due to the greater dependency of some previously independent emotional countries, a price paid for economic recovery. This analysis proved the usefulness of distinguishing four domains of socio-economic development and the application of this distinction in further studies (Table 5.1).

Assuming that group of independent rational countries is the most desirable from socio-economic development point of view, one might expect that governments and power elites would be pushing in this direction by designing and implementing convenient strategies. The BDI analysis shows that this is not the case. As it was mentioned above, people are not particularly fond of long range strategies aimed at the magnificent (distant) future. They prefer instant gratification and, in particular, the avoidance of temporary inconveniences. That's why architects of successful reforms in Germany, Spain and Poland paid a price by losing political support and power. Only real and present danger and/or idealistic motivation can make politicians pay such a price. The lack of the interdisciplinary BDI type of analysis is also visible. "Pure" economists using their quantitative models and separated by high walls from other social sciences, mainly sociology and political science, can only design future social and political disasters.

Table 5.1 Four types of economies in different periods

	2011	2014	2017
Dependent emotional	Greece	Greece Italy Portugal Spain	Ireland Greece Portugal Italy Spain Slovak Republic
Dependent rational	Ireland Poland	Ireland Poland	Poland
Independent emotional	Estonia Slovak Republic Czech Republic Latvia Italy Slovenia Netherlands Portugal Denmark Spain United Kingdom Hungary	Estonia Slovak Republic Slovenia Czech Republic Latvia United Kingdom Netherlands Denmark Hungary	Estonia Slovenia Latvia Czech Republic Hungary United Kingdom Netherlands
Independent rational	Austria France Sweden Luxembourg Belgium Finland Germany	France Austria Finland Sweden Luxembourg Belgium Germany	France Luxembourg Austria Germany Denmark Finland Sweden Belgium

2 Inroads into the Theory of Economic Cycles and Development

The construction and analysis of the Balanced Development Index can contribute to contemporary debate about the origins and the ways out of the economic crisis of 2007–2013. It shows that not only "hard" economic factors (such as changes in capital, labor and technical progress) create short-term and long-term economic changes, but these changes are also influenced by a number of social factors included in the BDI – social expectations and subjective assessment of the current economic and social situation. Such an approach goes beyond the traditional business cycle analysis. It is particularly fruitful in analyzing the short term changes, a subject belonging to the heart of the dispute in economic theory. Representatives of "hard" schools, the neo classical economy and, above all, the theory of the real business cycle, disregard the distinction between the long and short period. They believe that the business cycle mainly affects changes in capital, work and technical progress. Keynesians and representatives of behavioral economics, the new monetary theory or even the Austrian school point out that, in the short term, factors other than "hard" on the supply side, namely financial processes and actions of the state, can significantly affect the business cycle. The analysis of the BDI indicator shows, however, that in both the short and long term an important role modifying the business cycle may be played by social factors, better understood by sociology than by economics. Let us briefly recall the arguments of the main actors of this dispute.

As we have already mentioned, Michał Kalecki (1943a, b), who used not only economic indicators but also social and political factors, including the political cycle, played the pioneering role in the analysis of the business cycle mechanism. For Kalecki, the tensions between economic and social factors are limited to tensions between "capital and labor." Kalecki seeks to combine Keynesian and Marxist analyses. Many neo-socialists (Atkinson and Piketty 2010; Atkinson 2015), but also representatives of the "new pragmatism," (Kołodko 2014) are now returning to this idea in their battle against the neoliberals. However, the analysis of the BDI reveals that these tensions are even more complex, meaning that the analyses of Kalecki and his successors is significantly limited and may only partially serve as inspiration.

At the beginning of the twenty-first century, "behavioral economics" became very influential. This sometimes refers to Keynes, especially to his presentation of the role of the mental states of businessmen in the shaping of cyclical phases, with the special role of "irrational" or even "animal" expectations (Akerloff and Schiller 2010).

The research into the various domains of behavioral economics is undoubtedly very useful in our analysis. It is certainly worth using the research conclusions of G. Akerloff and R. Shiller (2010). They demonstrate that markets are not guided by balance-seeking price arbitration mechanisms, but by prices – especially the prices of various types of assets – which change under the influence of emotional, social and psychological factors such as: confidence and its multipliers, fairness, corruption and bad faith, money illusion, and stories.

Let us emphasize that "antisocial" schools of thought – such as neoclassical macroeconomics or the real business-cycle theory – also include economic actors such as: entrepreneurs and consumers in their economic analyses of the business cycle. Neoclassical macroeconomics classifies the expectations of economic actors as: rational, adaptive, extrapolative, or irrational in nature. These are very general categories. Our contribution is the use of the results of sociological research directly responding to questions regarding what people expect in the future for themselves, their family, their company, their country. In such a way both assessments of the current situation and expectations for the future take on a concrete form of emotionally loaded human judgments and feelings to be directly confronted with a hard economic reality as it is described by classical and neoclassical economists. We propose a mix of social and economic research.

The above arguments lead us to a concept of socioeconomic development, which treats economic and social factors as equally important. Consequently, this leads to the concept of a complex development index, whose partial economic and social components – "lower tier" indicators – receive equal statistical weight.

However, the representatives of the new classical macroeconomics (Lucas 1981; Barro 1974; Sims 1972; Sargent and Wallace 1975) assume that, in the long range, markets balance themselves and clear excess supply and demand, including labor markets. Thus unemployment emerges as voluntary because everyone willing to work may find a job if they agreed to an appropriate wage, which is usually much too low. Micro economic actors are characterized by rational expectations and they can optimize their behaviors. Our research shows that such an oversimplified view inhibits the understanding of short business cycles having a much stranger impact on people's lives. Emotions based on imperfect information and human hopes, aspirations, fears and prejudices must also be taken into consideration and the BDI index allows for that. It demonstrates how individual actors' irrationality, or imperfect rationality, is being projected by a political process onto much larger structures such individual countries leading sovereign, or intended as sovereign socio-economic policies.

Similarly, the proponents of the real business-cycle theory (Kydland and Prescott 1982) seek to place macroeconomics on an even stronger classical (supply-side) foundation. According to them, micro economic actors strive to maximize profits, shape their expectations in a purely rational way, while price flexibility ensures market cleaning. Employment fluctuations result from a voluntary change in the number of working hours people want to offer (as work and leisure are highly interchangeable). These authors reject the distinction between long and short periods. The key point is that changes in the pace of technological progress are subject to large irregular fluctuations. Conversely, on the supply side, these changes (shocks) via the macroeconomic function of production cause shifts in production and employment. Our main point is that economic actors, even collective ones, such as companies, are people. And people are subjective in their judgments and emotional in their choices. In the BDI model, the hard economic reality is reflected in people's minds and souls.

Therefore, the excessive "hard" economization of social problems in the neoclassical macroeconomics or in the real business-cycle theory makes it necessary for their proponents to cling to the concept of rational expectations. It enables the creation of sophisticated models but demonstrates a weak ability to explain the actual dynamics of tensions between economic and social factors. We seek to capture these tensions with our study of the functional balance measured by the BDI index. The concept of the functional balance allows to bring the notion of controllability of large socio-economic systems, or in other words, their proneness of being controlled or restructured from a decision center, into the picture. A low BDI implies the necessity of such an intervention, but makes it difficult and thorny. A high BDI makes it easier but the necessity of such moves is not generally felt. Economics is intertwined here with politics and management. The BDI makes the necessity of such an interdisciplinary approach even more evident and provides some kind of platform for it. Such an approach should enable to detect when a window of opportunity for reforms opens and when they become indispensable for the future development of the system. The BDI analysis can help to design the most socially and politically feasible reform path on the foundations of the empirical knowledge of people's emotions, opinions and aspirations.

On the other hand, in the abundant social sciences literature some excessively sociological approaches can be found as well. Such literature underestimates or even neglects hard economic factors influencing social dynamics and tensions. A good example is classic M. Weber's (1973) concept of the distribution of dignity and the role of religion, O. Hirschman's (1977) idea of development economics, or concept of integral development introduced by F. Perroux (1981). Without introducing economic factors and without an understanding of the economic logic of the business cycle, one is not able to explain a good life, flourishing, happiness, or welfare. One sided approaches found in the sharing economy or social economics do not provide adequate explanations and realistic projects for the future. A neoclassical touch is needed along with sociological data, not just abstract concepts.

Creational expectations of large groups of population can produce such dramatic outcomes as Brexit or the upcoming "trade war" between the US and China. The fact that such expectations are based on false premises and all kinds of fake news should not discourage researchers. In order to explain, understand and control any social reality, it should be analyzed as it is, not disregarded as "false" "prejudicial" etc.

The growth of emotional social expectations is becoming a new megatrend in the global economy, next to technological, financial and management megatrends (business models). The media narrative plays a huge role in their consolidation in the world, including the Internet narrative and unchartered seas of social media. The origins and influence of mental megatrends is widely analyzed in the literature, both sociological and economic (see: Baker et al. 2015; Gulen and Ion 2015; Akey and Lewellen 2017). The consequences of political uncertainty are discussed not only after Brexit, but above all after the election of D. Trump, and also after every political change in many countries around the world. As we have already pointed out emotional chaos remains the main driver of these changes so deep and rapid that even financial markets are taken by surprise.

BDI can often be better than any other harbinger of economic change broadly understood as a socio-economic and political climate. None of its components should be analyzed in isolation from others. Thanks to such a comprehensive interdisciplinary analysis, it is possible to resolve the age-old dispute between economists. To put it in a nutshell: in the emotional economies "govern": John M. Keynes (1936), George Akerlof, Robert Shiller, Paul Krugman (2011), Olivier Blanchard or Stephanie Kelton and in rational economies "govern": Robert Lucas, Robert Barro, Edward Prescott, Fin Kydland or Wolfgang Schäuble (2011).

The changes in social expectations occurring in the "middle" countries, i.e. moderately "independent" and "emotional", are a particularly important research field. In these countries we shall selectively apply both academic "schools of thought" about economy and socio-economic policy. As for now, "countries in the middle" are trying to become similar to the leading rational German economy, but social, political and theoretical changes can also move these countries towards dependent and emotional ones.

The economic crisis of 2007–2013 created a necessity to reconsider previously established paradigms of the theory of economics. The key theoretical works that make up an informal program of rebuilding the economic paradigm have been written by: D. Diamond and R. Dybvig (1983), R. Thaler and C. Sunstein (2009), J. Gali

(2015), G. Mankiw (1985), M. Woodford (2011), G. Akerloff and J. Yelen (1990), B. Bernanke (1990), B. Holmstrom and J. Tirole (1997), J. Taylor (1993), P. Romer (1994), P. Aghion and P. Howitt (1990), A. Shleifer and R. Vichny (1997), B. Hall and C. I. Jones (1999), S. Fischer (1993), L. Kotlikoff (2010), S. Kelton (2015), H. F. Mynski (1882), R. Dornbusch and S. Edwards (1989), D. Acemoglu et al. (2005). These landmark works open the space to use such research tools as the BDI, exposing social expectations, a functional balance and system control in the analysis of business cycles. The advantage of democratic and rational economies over the emotional and undemocratic ones is clearly shown in the works of D. Acemoglu and his colleagues (2005). Their conclusions are very similar to the results of our research.

When analyzing the crises focus on the "autonomous" role of financial markets, most globally recognized contemporary economists focus on the banking system and the central bank. The main trends in economic analysis do not include social expectations, a functional balance and system control. They do not pay attention to social expectations that have forced the US administration and the FED to support the artificial economic bubble based on subprime loans. People expected some kind of support of their consumption aspirations even when they had no credentials required by rigorous credit regimes. That's why the state controlled financial institutions gave the green light: "a home for everyone" program. The government was trying in such a way to resolve the problem of compromised functional balance due to the inability to satisfy creational expectations of the people. Speculative financial markets perceived that as an opportunity, and the subprime financial crisis exploded compromising the functional equilibrium even further. Such unprecedented measures as massive Quantitative Easing were needed to restore it and to meet the new wave of creational expectations.

Against the background of the above reconstruction of economic theory, we can summarize our approach and our contribution to this debate in the form of the following diagram (Fig. 5.1).

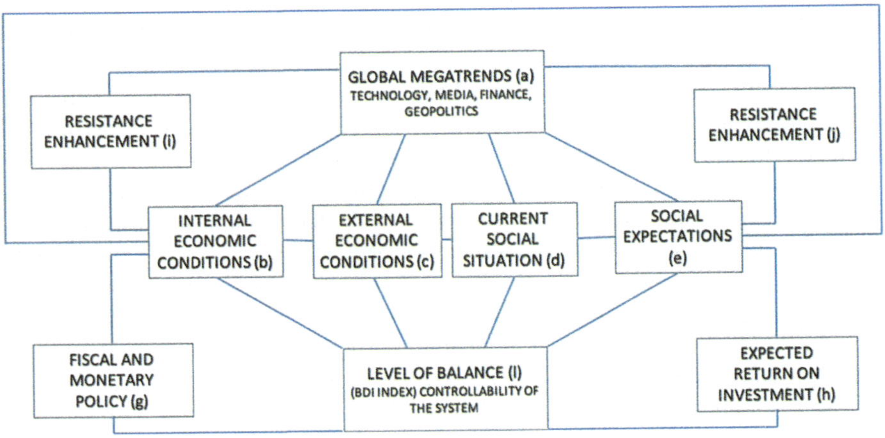

Fig. 5.1 Determinants of the functional balance

Figure 5.1 represents general outlook of relationships (feedback loops) between key determinants of the functional balance as measured by the BDI. Fiscal and monetary policies are the only "instruments" in the hands of governments, ruling elites, policy makers etc. Such instruments trigger resistance or sometimes support enhancement. Other factors influencing the balance are highly subjective and often emotional. The expected return on investment falls into that category along with subjective perception of global megatrends.

The most relevant feedbacks presented in Fig. 5.1 are following:

1. The loop between "l" and "b" (between the level of balance and the internal economic situation of a country) is intermediated by government policies: monetary, fiscal and in the longer run, industrial and institutional. Governments can use such policies to improve the compromised balance (in a recession or crisis situation) or consciously decrease the level of balance in order to kick off development. Government policies have an impact on savings (of households, enterprises and other organizations) and the propensity to invest, as well as imports, exports and the inflow of foreign capital.
2. The loop between "l" (the level of balance) and "e" (social expectations) is fundamentally social in nature. The loop is intermediated by consumer confidence, propensity to save, to invest and to undertake entrepreneurial and innovative activities. Emotions play a key role. People's hopes and expectations are influenced by main-stream and social media spreading propaganda, fake or exaggerated news, false or exaggerated promises, panic and enthusiasm. That's why the relationship between expectations and socio-economic balance is unstable and the most dynamic of all. It has the most powerful potential to change the level of equilibrium, to inhibit or enhance the controllability of the system. As a result it has become the main field of political games.
3. The loop linking "e", "h" and "l" is particularly interesting because it demonstrates the key role of investments as a factor influencing the level of socio-economic balance. Investments are understood broadly, including not only entrepreneurs and stock market participants, but also people investing in their own homes or apartments, education, health, children's future etc. High expectations increase the expected rate of return on all kinds of investments and make them happen, improving the level of socio-economic balance. This is a typical example of positive feedback.
4. Social and economic government policies trigger all kinds of reactions from business, public opinion, politicians and sometime foreign actors of the same sorts. Such reactions ("a", "I" and "J" on the Fig. 5.1) can translate into either enhancement or resistance to policies. Government policies are blocked or reinforced in such a way. Quite often conflicting forces of that kind are at play and the final outcome remains uncertain.

Changes of expectations are correlated with political changes bringing about new policies. The explanation is twofold:

- When political change occurs people expect improvements;

- Expectations, which do not come true bring about disillusionment and increase pressure for political change.

Radical and comprehensive policy and institutional changes (reforms) should be undertaken in quiet times of a relatively high degree (but not maximum) of dynamic balance. Material reserves and the popular acceptance of authorities make them easier. In reality reforms are implemented in turbulent times of compromised equilibrium putting the political status quo in jeopardy or even crushing it into pieces.

3 Policy Implications

Before we move to the policy implications of the BDI analysis we have to get rid of the simplistic assumption that there is an Omniscient Planner or some other Hegemon "up there", who makes rational policy decisions on the grounds of the state of the art knowledge and a thorough expert analysis of all the available information. As Nobel Prize winner Robert Solow points out in his 2008 testimony in front of The House Committee of Science and Technology, such an unrealistic "Big Brother" assumption corresponds well with the mainstream macroeconomic models of the dynamic stochastic general equilibrium (DSGE): "*They take it for granted that the whole economy can be thought about as if it were a single, consistent person or dynasty carrying out a rationally designed, long-term plan, occasionally disturbed by unexpected shocks, but adapting to them in a rational, consistent way*" (Bookstaber 2017: 92). We demonstrated in our BDI analysis that policies cannot be purely rational because they result from collective emotions and are being developed under the strong influence of volatile political games.

We firstly have to understand that policies concern the future. And as Karl Popper (1990: 17–18) puts it: "*Quite apart from the fact that we do not know the future, the future is objectively not fixed. The future is open: objectively open*". Policies shape the future in real time and because of that they cannot be fixed either. They are constantly adjusted as the future emerges from the present under conditions of "radical uncertainty" (Bookstaber 2017) or "generalized uncertainty". Such conditioning spells out the impossibility of calculating the risks: political risks in first order, but also financial, economic, social, etc. All of them, however, can be translated into the language of politics. And political actors play a fast ball game. That's why policy making is about agility: the constant disposition to adjust or change not only instruments, but objectives of policies, quite often in irrational emotional ways. Policies around the "Brexit mess" provide an example of such a situation.

The BDI analysis gives an insight into one part of the emerging process of policy making: the interplay between four components of the index: external and internal economic conditions, social assessment of current conditions and expectations for the future. Each one of these elements can be used as a playing card by politicians and is transported to social consciousness by the media narrative capable of turning success into failure and failure into success. To some degree of course. We did not inquire into political and media games. We simply assume that these processes exist, and they are capable of changing the picture. To some degree of course. In the long range, the logic of interplay between four BDI components is likely to prevail. Its analysis indicates key sources of disharmony in the system and the most efficient ways to keep them within the range of safety preventing the system from the loss of controllability, and at the same time from stagnation. Being technically right is not enough, however, whoever uses such an analytic tool in policy making practice, needs to command well-orchestrated political and media support. Otherwise good ideas remain in the world of abstraction.

The BDI analysis sheds new light on one of the fundamental issues of economic policy: when and in what circumstances serious structural reforms should be undertaken in order to secure survival and the future development of the system?. Social expectations are capable of enforcing such a specific, radical policy when people realize that they are really needed, when popular economic imagination reaches a higher level of rationality. German and Spanish reforms were undertaken under such circumstances. Due to the different content of public opinion expectations, and perhaps because of the lack of determination or political skills of the ruling coalition, such structural reforms were not undertaken in France or in Poland in 2007–2015. Reforms are possible in purely economic terms, where there is space for lowering interest rates, for intensifying credit creation, and for increasing budget deficits and public debt. These are not sufficient conditions, however, creative expectations must be in line with the reform projects. And such expectations can empirically identified and described. In such a way, the BDI research and empirical sociology move the economic policy debate from abstract to concrete.

The BDI analysis enables three different approaches to the issue of maintaining and improving socio-economic balance of the system to be identified.

1. The first approach is aimed at improving the valuation of the current situation and building up positive creative expectations by flooding the economy and households with money. Such a typically Keynesian policy can be implemented through ambitious public projects (infrastructure, transportation, energy, housing, etc.) and massive social welfare transfers. Such measures are financed by deficit state spending and mounting public debt. Since these policies are generally well received by the public, social acceptance and optimistic expectations rise as they are implemented. A policy shift becomes needed when the deficit slips out of control and production as well as productivity growth are halted. The shift is therefore more and more difficult since populist politics supporting that kind of economic policy, plays on high emotions and more and more ambitious creative expectations. The choice of such an approach to socio-economic equilibrium is most likely in a good economic climate, when the economy is performing well. If spending goes too far, some kind of stagflation trap opens. After 2015, Poland chose that kind of approach because of purely political reasons. It brought to power new ruling elites.

2. The second approach takes advantage of a difficult, or at least a subjectively worsening economic situation: high unemployment, slow productivity and GDP growth, mounting pessimism etc. This situation can become an opportunity to persuade public opinion that proactive structural changes are needed in order to build up a country's competitive advantage and to successfully face the upcoming crisis. Public spending cuts, deregulation of the labor markets and the rationalization of welfare policies are usually on such an agenda. The success of such a policy depends on lowering the level of emotions and uplifting the rationality of social assessment of the current situation and expectations for the future, but also the quality of public management and political class. This worked in Germany and Spain, but it did not in France and in Italy.
3. The third approach is based on two pillars: massive investment in education, science, technology, ecology and health and the rationalization of the state's and households' revenues and expenses, for example, through the conversion of social benefits into tax cuts. Investment drive directed towards human and other intangible assets is aimed at triggering spillover effects according to the endogenous growth models (by Romer 1994; Aghion and Howitt 1990). Such an approach is possible in affluent well educated deeply democratic societies, where emotions and expectations remain on the rational side. Elements of this approach can be found in Scandinavian countries: Denmark, Finland, Sweden.

The choice of one of the three approaches can be based on the BDI analysis, during which the inertia of social moods and emotions, institutions and culture are taken into consideration. The diagnosis of the social fabric is more important and more difficult than financial engineering. Both should go hand in hand.

Policy making has always been under the influence of the emotions of its main stakeholders, including policy makers and supporting (promoting) politicians, various interest groups and lobbies (including business related), general public and public opinion segments, economists, experts consultants, foreign partners (public and private). We are not in a position to delve into the nature of collective emotions. We just assume that emotions related to policy making can be both "positive" (like: hope, ambition, greed etc.) and "negative" (like: fear, envy, panic, despair etc.) and that they serve as mobilization triggers directing groups of actors for or against concrete policies. Politicians play with collective emotions using media and information technologies. Due to previously unhreard technological leverage, collective emotions became the main battlefield of power wars. It directly affects policy making. Our comparative longitudinal analysis of BDI dynamics shows that policies are becoming increasingly emotional and more and more countries are drifting towards the dark, emotional side of our four pole typology.

Up to recently, however, emotions were successfully moderated by professional policy makers, civil servants and intellectual elites, acting on behalf of the common good and respecting state of the art knowledge and factual evidence. In the last decade or so this common thread of rationality was mauled. Elites lost their credibility because they were not able to live up to the inflated expectation of large groups of the population loosing grounds to globalization and technology forces.

At the same time thousands of false prophets appeared in the net. Dissatisfaction was mercilessly exploited and overblown by aspiring political forces, who seem to have lost common good and rationality from sight. As we have demonstrated, emotions and rationality are presently co-determining the emergence of policies. Which ones will prevail? There is no safe bet on either of them.

Bibliography

Acemoglu D, Johnson S, Robinson J (2005) Institutions as a fundamental cause of long-run growth. In: Handbook of economic growth. North-Holland, Amsterdam
Aghion P, Howitt P (1990) A model of growth through creative destruction. No. w3223. National Bureau of Economic Research
Akerlof GA, Shiller RJ (2010) Animal spirits: how human psychology drives the economy, and why it matters for global capitalism. Princeton University Press, Princeton
Akerlof GA, Yellen JL (1990) The fair wage-effort hypothesis and unemployment. Q J Econ 105:2
Akey P, Lewellen S (2017) Policy uncertainty, political capital, and firm risk-taking. Political capital, and firm risk-taking, March 22, 2017
Algan Y (2018) Trust and social capital. In: Stiglitz J, Fitousi JP, Durand M (eds) For good measure – advancing research on well-being metrics beyond GDP. OECD, Paris
Allardt E (1993) Having, loving, being: an alternative to the Swedish model of welfare research. In: Nussbaum MA and Sen A (eds) The quality of life, 8. Clarendon Press, Oxford, pp 88–95
Arechavala NS, Espina PZ, Tropero BP (eds) (2015) The economic crisis and its effects on the quality of life in the European Union. Soc Indic Res 120:323–343
Artus P, Broyer S (2013) France-Allemagne: une comparaison des effets de gamme dans l'industrie. Rev Econ Ind (144):59–84
Atkinson A (2015) Inequalities. What can be done? Harvard University Press, Cambridge, MA
Atkinson A, Piketty T (2010) Top incomes. A global perspective. Oxford University Press, Oxford
Atkinson T, Cantillon B, Marlier E, Nolan B (2002) Social indicators: the EU and social inclusion. OUP, Oxford
Baker SR, Bloom N, Davis SJ (2015) Measuring economic policy uncertainty, NBER working paper, Cambridge, MA
Balcerowicz L (1995) Socialism, capitalism, transformation. Central European University Press, Budapest
Barro RJ (1974) Are government bonds net wealth? J Polit Econ 82:6
Barro RJ, Sala-i-Martin X (2003) Economic growth. MacGraw Hill, New York
Bauer RA (ed) (1966) Social indicators. MIT Press, Cambridge
Berenger V, Veredier-Chouchane A (2007) Multidimensional measures of Well-being: standard of living and quality of life across countries. World Dev 35(7):1259–1276
Bericat E, Jiménez-Rodrigo ML (2019) The quality of European societies – A compilation of composite indicators. Springer, Cham

A. K. Koźmiński et al., *The Balanced Development Index for Europe's OECD Countries, 1999–2017*, SpringerBriefs in Economics,
https://doi.org/10.1007/978-3-030-39240-6

Brieitkopf M, Jaszczyński D, Górski M (1991) Privatization in Poland. Verelag nicht Ermittelbar, Berlin

Bernanke B (1990) The federal funds rate and the channels of monetary transmission no. w3487. National Bureau of Economic Research

BES (2014) Il benessere equo esastenbile in Italia. Cnel-Istat, Roma

Bilbao-Ubillos J (2013) Another approach to measuring human development: the composite dynamic human development index. Soc Indic Res 111(2):473–484

Blanchard O (2015, July) Greece: past critiques and the path forward'. iMFdirect. In: The International Monetary Fund's global economy forum, vol 9

Bookstaber R (2017) The end of theory. Financial crises, the failure of economics and the sweep of human interaction. Princeton University Press, Princeton/Oxford

Brulé G, Suter Ch (2019) Wealth(s) and subjective well-being. Springer, Cham

Buchanan JM, Tullock G (1962) The calculus of consent, vol 3. University of Michigan Press, Ann Arbor

Buscha F (2012) Financial expectations and the 'left–right'political value scale: testing for the POUM hypothesis. Econ Lett 115(3):460–464

Carabelli A, Cedrini M (2011) The economic problem of happiness: Keynes on happiness and economics. For Soc Econ 40(3):335–359. Taylor & Francis Group

Carnap R (1962) Logical foundations of probability. University of Chicago Press, Chicago

Cassell D, Cichy EV (1987) The growing shadow economy in socialist planning systems: causes and consequences. Nauki o Zarządzaniu 1:49–63

Cavaleri S, Obloj K (1993) Management Systems. Wadsworth Publishing Co, Belmont Cal

Clark AE, Senik C (2011) Will GDP growth increase subjective happiness in developing countries? In: Measure for measure how well do we measure development?: proceedings of the 8th AFD-EUDN conference.(3) 2011; 8. Conference AFD-EUDN. Measure for measure: how well do we measure development? FRA, Paris. 2010-12-01, 97-176. AFD-Agence Française de Développement

Clark AE, Senik C (eds) (2014) Happiness and economic growth: lessons from developing countries. Oxford University Press, Oxford

Cohen WJ (1968) Social indicators: statistics for public policy. Am Stat 22(4):14–16

Cojocaru A (2014) Prospects of upward mobility and preferences for redistribution: evidence from the Life in Transition Survey. Eur J Polit Econ 34:300–314

Costanza R, Hart M, Talberth J, Posner S (2009) Beyond GDP: the need for new measures of progress. In: The pardee papers 4. Pardee Center for the Study of the Longer-Range Future, Boston

Cummins RA, Eckersley R, Pallant J, Van Vugt J, Misajon R (2003) Developing a national index of subjective wellbeing: the Australian Unity wellbeing index. Soc Indic Res 64(2):159–190

Davino C, Dolce P, Taralli S, Vinzi VE (2018) A quantile composite-indicator approach for the measurement of equitable and sustainable well-being: a case study of the italian provinces. Soc Indic Res 136(3):999–1029

de Bustillo RM, Antón JI (2015) Turning Back before arriving: the weakening of the Spanish welfare state. In: The European social model in crisis: is Europe losing its soul? Edward Elgar, Cheltenham

Delhey J, Böhnke P, Habich R, Zapf W (2002) Quality of life in a European perspective: the EUROMODULE as a new instrument for comparative welfare research. In: Assessing quality of life and living conditions to guide National Policy. Springer, Dordrecht, pp 163–176

Di Tella R, MacCulloch R (2006) Some uses of happiness data in economics. J Econ Perspect 20(1):25–46

Di Tella RD, MacCulloch RJ, Oswald AJ (2003) The macroeconomics of happiness. Rev Econ Stat 85(4):809–827

Diamond DW, Dybvig PH (1983) Bank runs, deposit insurance, and liquidity. J Polit Econ 91(3):401–419

Diener E (1995) A value based index for measuring national quality of life. Soc Indic Res 36(2):107–127

Diener E, Seligman ME (2004) Beyond money: toward an economy of Well-being. Psychol Sci Public Interest 5(1):1–31. University of Illinois
Diener E, Suh E (1997) Measuring quality of life: economic, social, and subjective indicators. Soc Indic Res 40(1–2):189–216
Dijkstra AG (2002) Revisiting UNDP's GDI and GEM: towards an alternative. Soc Indic Res 57(3):301–338
Dillard DD (1948) Economics of John Maynard Keynes. Prentice-Hall, New York
Dolado JJ, García-Serrano C, Jimeno JF (2002) Drawing lessons from the boom of temporary jobs in Spain. Econ J 112(480):F270
Dornbusch R, Edwards S (1989) Macroeconomic populism in Latin America (no. w2986). National Bureau of Economic Research, Cambridge, MA
Drewnowski J (1970) Studies in the measurement of levels of living and welfare. United Nations Research Institute for Social Development, Geneva
Dutt AK, Radcliff B (eds) (2009) Happiness, economics and politics: towards a multi-disciplinary approach. Edward Elgar Publishing, Cheltenham
Easterlin RA (1974) Does economic growth improve the human lot? Some empirical evidence. In: Nations and households in economic growth. Academic, New York, pp 89–125
Easterlin RA (ed) (2002) Happiness in economics. Edward Elgar Publishing, Cheltenham
Ebert U, Welsch H (2004) Meaningful environmental indices: a social choice approach. J Environ Econ Manag 47(2):270–283
EBRD (European Bank for Reconstruction and Development) (1996) Transition Report
Espina PZ, Arechavala NS (2013) An assessment of social welfare in Spain: territorial analysis using a synthetic welfare indicator. Soc Indic Res 111(1):1–23
Estes RJ (1984) The social progress of nations. Praeger, New York, pp 1–179
Estes RJ (1988) Toward a 'quality-of-life'index: empirical approaches to assessing human welfare internationally. In: The third world: states of mind and being. Unwin Hyman, Boston, pp 23–36
Estes RJ (2019) The social progress of nations revisited, 1970–2020. Springer, Cham
Estes RJ, Morgan JS (1976) World social welfare analysis: a theoretical model. Int Soc Work 19(2):29–41
Festinger L (1962) A theory of cognitive dissonance, vol 2. Stanford University Press, Stanford
Fischer S (1993) The role of macroeconomic factors in growth. J Monet Econ 32(3):485–512
Fleurbaey M, Blanchet D (2013) Beyond GDP: measuring welfare and assessing sustainability. Oxford University Press, Oxford
Fox KA (1977) Social indicators & social theory. Wiley, New York/London
Frey BS (2008) Happiness: a revolution in economics. MIT press, Cambridge, MA
Frey BS, Gallus J (2013) Political economy of happiness. Appl Econ 45(30):4205–4211
Frey BS, Stutzer A (2008) The thirst for happiness. J Int Bus Ethics 1(1):8–17
Galbraith J (1958) Theaffluent society, V Boston Houghton Miffl, Boston
Galbraith JK (2016) Welcome to the poisoned chalice: the destruction of Greece and the future of Europe. Yale University Press, New Haven
Gali J (2015) Monetary policy, inflation, and the business cycle. An introduction to the new Keynesian framework and its applications. Princeton University Press, Princeton/Oxford
Galtung J (1976) Towards new indicators of development. Futures 8(3):261–265
Gaskarth G (2014) The Hartz reforms... And their lessons for the UK. Centre for Policy Studies, London
Giesselmann M, Hilmer R, Siegel NA, Wagner GG (2013) Measuring well-being: W3 indicators to complement GDP. DIW Econ Bull 5:10–19
Gobierno de Espana, Minsterio de la Presidencia (2012) Reforms by the Government of Spain, Combating the crisis with determination, Madrid
Greco S, Ishizaka A, Tasiou M, Torrisi G (2019) On the methodological framework of composite indices: a review of the issues of weighting, aggregation, and robustness. Soc Indic Res 141(1):61–94
Guardiola J, Picazo-Tadeo A, Rojas M (2014) Economic crisis and well-being in Europe: introduction. Soc Indic Res Published online first 120:2

Gulen H, Ion M (2015) Policy uncertainty and corporate investment. Rev Financ Stud 29:3
Hagerty MR, Cummins RA, Ferris AL, Land K, Michalos AC, Peterson M (2001) Quality of life indexes for national policy: review and agenda for research. Bull Sociolog Method/Bulletin de Méthodologie Sociologique 71(1):58–78
Hall RE, Jones CI (1999) Why do some countries produce so much more output per worker than others? Q J Econ 114(1):83–116
Hausmann R et al (2013) The atlas of economic complexity. Mapping paths to prosperity. Massachusetts Institute of Technology and Center for International Development, Harvard University, Cambridge, MA/London
Helliwell JF, Layard PR, Sachs J (eds) (2018) World happiness report 2018. Sustainable Development Solutions Network, New York
Hirschman AO (1977) The passions and the interests. Political arguments for capitalism before its triumph. Princeton University Press, New Jersey
Hirschman AO (1981) Essays in trespassing: economics to politics and beyond. Cambridge University Press, Cambridge
Holmstrom B, Tirole J (1997) Financial intermediation, loanable funds, and the real sector. Q J Econ 112(3):663–691
Huppert FA, So TT (2013) Flourishing across Europe: application of a new conceptual framework for defining well-being. Soc Indic Res 110(3):837–861
Ivaldi E, Bonatti G, Soliani R (2016) The construction of a synthetic index comparing multidimensional well-being in the European Union. Soc Indic Res 125(2):397–430
Iversen T, Soskice D (2019) Democracy and prosperity: reinventing capitalism through a turbulent century. Princeton University Press, Princeton
Kaldor N (1940) A model of the trade cycle. Econ J 50:78
Kalecki M (1943a) Studies on economic dynamics. Allen & Unwin, London
Kalecki M (1943b) Political aspect of full employment. Polit Q XIV:322
Kanbur R, Patel E, Stiglitz J (2018) Sustainable development goals and measurement of economic and social progress. For good measure: advancing research on well-being metrics beyond GDP, 33. OECD, Paris
Kaplan SR, Norton PD (1996) Balanced scorecard: translating strategy into action. Harvard Business School Press, Cambridge. What is business organizing for, 51
Kelton S (2015) 2. The failure of austerity: rethinking fiscal policy. Polit Q 86:28–46
Kentor J (2001) The long term effects of globalization on income inequality, population growth, and economic development. Soc Probl 48(4):435–455
Keynes JM (1936) The general theory of employment, interest and money (1936). Kessinger Publishing, Whitefish
Keynes JM (1971) Letter to Roy Harrod (4 July 1938) in: The collected writings of John Maynard Keynes, vol XIV. Macmillan, London
Kingdon JW (1995) Agendas, alternatives, and public policies, 2nd edn. Longman, New York
Kluve J, Jacobi L (2006) Before and after the Hartz Reforms: the performance of active labor market policy in Germany. Rheinisch-Westflisches Institut fr Wirtschaftsforschung RWI Discussion Papers, 41
Kołodko GW (2000) From shock to therapy: the political economy of postsocialist transformation. Oxford University Press, New York
Kołodko GW (2002) Globalization and catching-up in transition economies. University of Rochester Press, Rochester/Woodbridge/Suffolk
Kołodko G (2011) Truth, errors, and lies: politics and economics in a volatile world. Columbia University Press, New York
Kołodko G (2014) The new pragmatism, or economics and policy for the future: (an essay). Acta Oecon 64(2):139–160
Kołodko GW (2016) How to destroy a country. The economics and the politics of the Greek crisis. (September 14, 16)
Kołodko GW (2017) New pragmatism: in the quest for economics and development policy in the 21st century. J Manag Bus Admin Central Eur 25(2):2–5

Koralewicz J, Zagórski K (2009) Living conditions and optimistic orientation of Poles. Int J Soc 39(4):10–44

Kotlikoff LJ (2010) Jimmy Stewart is dead: ending the World's ongoing financial plague with limited purpose banking. Wiley, Hoboken

Koźmiński AK (1988) Reformer l'economie socialiste: les perspectives Polonaises. Revue d'études Comparatives Est-Ouest 19(4):47–69

Koźmiński AK (1993) Catching up?: organizational and management change in the ex-socialist block. Suny Press, Albany

Koźmiński AK (2008) How it all happened: essays in political economy of transition. Difin, Warsaw

Koźmiński AK, Noga A, Piotrowska K, Zagórski K (2014) Kozminski University index of balanced economic and social development. In: Kołodko GW (ed) Management and economic policy for development. Nova Science Publishers, New York, pp 251–270

Koźmiński AK, Noga A, Piotrowska K, Zagórski K (2015) Operationalization and estimation of balanced development index for Poland 1999–2016. Stat Trans, Spring 16(1):1–18

Koźmiński AK, Noga A, Piotrowska K, Zagórski K (2016) The balanced develpment index: its construction and application in times of uncertainty Poland 1999–2017. Pol Sociolog Rev 3(95):267–289

Krafft M, Perring-Chiello P, Walker AM (eds) (2018) Hope for a good life: Results of the hope-barometer international research program. Springer, Cham

Krebs T, Scheffel M (2013) German labour reforms: unpopular success. Recuperado de http://voxeu.org/article/germanlabour-reforms-unpopular-success

Krugman P (2011) Keynes was right. New York Times 29:A23

Kuznets S (1934) National Income 1929–32: a report to the U.S. senate, 73rd congress, 2nd session. US Government Printing Office, Washington

Kydland FE, Prescott EC (1982) Time to build and aggregate fluctuations. Econometrica 50:1345–1370

Land KC, Felson M (1976) A general framework for building dynamic macro social indicator models: including an analysis of changes in crime rates and police expenditures. Am J Sociol 82(3):565–604

Land KC, Michalos AC (2018) Fifty years after the social indicators movement: has the promise been fulfilled? Soc Indic Res 135(3):835–868

Landels DS (2015) Wealth and poverty of nations. Why some are so rich and others so poor. W.W. Norton & Company, New York

Lee E, Vivarelli M (2006) The social impact of globalization in the developing countries. Int Labour Rev 145(3):167–184

Li Q, Reuveny R (2003) Economic globalization and democracy: an empirical analysis. Br J Polit Sci 33(1):29–54

Lin JY, Monga C, Standaert S (2019) The inclusive sustainable transformation index. Soc Indic Res 143(1):47–80

Lucas RE (1981) Studies in business theory. Basil Blackwell, Oxford

Lustig N (2018) Measuring the distribution of household income, consumption and wealth. In: Stiglitz JE, Fitoussi JP, Durand M (eds) For good measure – advancing research on well-being metrics beyond GDP. OECD, Paris

Lyapunov AM (1992) The general problem of the stability of motion. Taylor & Francis, London UK. English translation

Madonia G, Cracolicci MF i, Cuffaro M (2013) Exploring wider wellbeing in the EU 15 countries. An empirical application of the Stiglitz report. Soc Indic Res 111:117–140

Malewski A (1962) Two models of sociology. Pol Sociolog Bull 1-2/3-4:17–27

Mankiw GN (1985) Consumer durables and the real interest rate. Rev Econ Stat 67:353

McGranahan DV, Richard-Proust C, Sovani NV, Subramanian M (1970) Content and measurement of socio-economic development – an empirical inquiry. United Nations Research Institute for Social Development Report Nr. 70.10, Geneva

Michalos AC (ed) (2014) Encyclopedia of quality of life and well-being research. Springer Netherlands, Dordrecht
Mills CW (1959/2000) The sociological imagination. Oxford University Press, Oxford
Morris MD (1980) The physical quality of life index. Dev Dig 18(1):95–109
Moser CA (1970) Measuring the quality of life. New Soc XII/1970:1042–1043
Moser CA (1973) Social indicators – systems, methods and problems. Rev Income Wealth 19(2):133–141
Mynski HF (1882) The financial instability hypothesis. The Jerome Levy Institute of Bard College Working Paper 73, Bilithewood
Naim M (2013) The end of power. From boardrooms to battlefields and churches, to states. Why being in charge Isn't what it used to be. Basic Books, New York
Natoli R, Zuhair S (2011) Measuring progress: a comparison of the GDP, HDI, GS and the RIE. Soc Indic Res 103(1):33–56
NEF, The New Economics Foundation (2009) The happy planet index. www.dowssx417g17s.cloudfront.net/nefoundation/defaultpage/-/files/happy-planet-index-report.pdf
Noga A (2016) Special theory of employment and co-productive goods. https://mpra.ub.uni-muenchen.de/78647/1/MPRA_paper_78647.pdf
Noll HH (2004) Social indicators and quality of life research: background, achievements and current trends. In: Advances in sociological knowledge. VS Verlag für Sozialwissenschaften, Wiesbaden, pp 151–181
Noll HH, Michalos AC (2014) International Sociological Association Working Group/Research Committee on social indicators. In: Encyclopedia of quality of life and well-being research. Springer, Heidelberg, pp 3331–3336
Nowak S (1977) Methodology of sociological research – general problems. Reidel, Dordrecht
OECD (2013) Better life index. OECD, Paris
OECD (2017) How is life? – 2017 – measuring well-being. OECD, Paris
OECD (2018) Spain –2018, overview-economic-survey
Offe C, Adler P (1991) Capitalism by democratic design? Democratic theory facing the triple transition in East Central Europe. Soc Res 58:865–892
Okun AM (1962) Potential GNP: its measurement and significance, Cowles Foundation Paper 190. Cowles Foundation, Yale University, New Haven
Pareto VA (1963) Treatise on general sociology, Doven Publications, New York
PARP (2018) Report on the state of the SME sector in Poland. Polish Agency for Enterprise Development, Warsaw
Pennock M, Ura K (2011) Gross national happiness as a framework for health impact assessment. Environ Impact Assess Rev 31(1):61–65
Perroux F (1981) Pour une philosophie du nouveau dévelopement, vol 4. Presses de l'UNESCO, Aubier
Piatkowski M (2018) Europe's growth champion: insights from the economic rise of Poland. Oxford University Press, Oxford
Piketty T (2014) Capital in the twenty-first century. The Belknap Press of Harvard University Press, Cambridge/Massachusetts/London
Popper KR (1959) The propensity interpretation of probability. Br J Philos Sci 10(37):25–42
Popper KR (1990) A world of propensities. Bristol, Thoemmes
Porter ME (1990) The competitive advantage of nations: with a new introduction. Free Press, New York
Porter ME, Stern S, Green M (2015) Social progress index 2015. Social Progress Imperative, Washington, DC. www.socialprogressimperative.org/system/resources
Powers C (2012) The role of sticking points in Pareto's theory of social systems, in: Femia JV and Marshall AJ (eds) Vilfredo Pareto: Beyond disciplinary boundaries. Ashgate, Surrey in Farnham
Ravallion M, Lokshin M (2000) Who wants to redistribute?: the tunnel effect in 1990s Russia. J Public Econ 76(1):87–104

Reig-Martínez E (2013) Social and economic wellbeing in Europe and the Mediterranean Basin: building an enlarged human development indicator. Soc Indic Res 111(2):527–547

Robertson R (1992) Globalization: social theory and global culture. Sage, London, p 16

Romer PM (1994) The origins of endogenous growth. J Econ Perspect 8(1):3–22

Saisana M, Tarantola S (2002) State-of-the-art report on current methodologies and practices for composite indicator development. European Commission, Joint Research Centre, Institute for the Protection and the Security of the Citizen, Technological and Economic Risk Management Unit, Ispra, p 214

Sargent TJ, Wallace N (1975) "Rational" expectations, the optimal monetary instrument, and the optimal money supply rule. J Polit Econ 83(2):241–254

Schäuble W (2011) Why austerity is only cure for the Eurozone. Financial Times 5(09):2011

Schepelmann P, Goossens Y, Makipaa A (2009) Towards sustainable development: alternatives to GDP for measuring progress (No. 42). Wuppertal Spezial

Sengenberger W (2002) Globalization and social progress: the role and impact of international labour standards, vol 9. Friedrich-Ebert-Stiftung, Bonn

Sheldon EB, Moore WE (1968) Indicators of social change: concepts and measurements. Russell Sage Foundation, New York

Shleifer A, Vishny RW (1997) A survey of corporate governance. J Financ 52(2):737–783

Sims CA (1972) Money, income, and causality. Am Econ Rev 62(4):540–552

Sirgy MJ (2011) Theoretical perspectives guiding QOL indicator projects. Soc Indic Res 103(1):1–22

Smits J, Steendijk R (2015) The international wealth index (IWI). Soc Indic Res 122(1):65–85

Stiglitz JE, Sen A, Fitoussi JP (2010) Mismeasuring our lives: why GDP doesn't add up. The New Press, New York

Stiglitz JE, Fitousi JP, Durand M (eds) (2018a) Beyond GDP – measuring what counts for economic and social performance. OECD, Paris

Stiglitz JE, Fitousi JP, Durand M (eds) (2018b) For good measure – advancing research on well-being metrics beyond GDP. OECD, Paris

Stone R (1966) Input-output and demographic accounting: a tool for educational planning. Minerva 4(3):365–380

Stone R (1971) An integrated system of demographic, manpower and social statistics and its links with the system of national economic accounts. Sankhyā Indian J Stat B 33:1–184

Streeck W (2016) How will capitalism end?: essays on a failing system. Verso Books, London

Summers L (2016a) The age of secular stagnation, foreign affairs, February 17

Summers L (2016b) A badly designed US stimulus will only hurt the working class. Financial Times, November 14

Taylor JB (1993) Discretion versus Policy Rules in Practice. Carnegie-Rochester conference series on public policy. Vol 39. North-Holland

Thaler RH, Sunstein CR (2009) Nudge: improving decisions about health, wealth, and happiness. Penguin, London

The Conference Board (2018) Leading economic index (LEI). https:///www.conference-board.org

Tuma NB, Hannan M (1984) Social dynamics: models and methods. Academic, New York

UN Statistical Office (1975) Towards a system of social and demographic statistics. New York: United Nations (Studies in Methods, Series F No. 18)

UNDP (2013) Human development index. UNDP, New York

UNDP (2018) Human development indices and indicators. UNDP, New York

UNESCO (1976) The use of socio-economic indicators in development planning. UNESCO Press, Paris

Ura K, Alkire S, Zangmo T, Wangdi K (2012) An extensive analysis of GNH index. http://www.grossnationalhappiness.com/wpcontent/uploads/2012/10/An%20Extensive%20Analysis%20of%20GNH%20Index.pdf

Van Praag BM, Van Praag B, Ferrer-i-Carbonell A (2004) Happiness quantified: a satisfaction calculus approach. Oxford University Press, Oxford
Varoufakis Y (2015) The global minotaur: America, Europe and the future of the global economy. Zed Books Ltd, London
Varoufakis Y (2017) Adults in the room: my battle with the European and American deep establishment. Farrar, Straus and Giroux, New York
Veenhoven R (1984) Conditions of happiness. D. Reidel, Dordrecht
Veenhoven R (2018) Co-development of happiness research: addition to "fifty years after the social indicator movement". Soc Indic Res 135(3):1001–1007
Veenhoven R, Ehrhardt J, Ho MSD, de Vries A (1993) Happiness in nations: subjective appreciation of life in 56 nations 1946–1992. Erasmus University Rotterdam, Rotterdam
Vogel SK (2018) Marketcraft: how governments make markets work. Oxford University Press, New York
Ward RE (ed) (2015) Political development in modern Japan: studies in the modernization of Japan. Princeton University Press, Princeton
Weber M (1973) The power of the state and the dignity of the academic calling in Imperial Germany: the writings of max Weber on university problems. Minerva 11:571–632
Weintraub ER (1974) General equilibrium theory. Macmillan, London
WHR (World Happiness Report 2019), Helliwell JF, Layard R, Sachs JD (2019) World happiness report 2019. Sustainable Development Solutions Network, New York
Wolf M (2014) The shifts and the shocks: what we've learned – and have still to learn – from the financial crisis. Penguin, New York
Woodford M (2011) Interest and prices: foundations of a theory of monetary policy. Princeton University Press, Princeton
Zagórski K (1975) Socio-demographic statistics in system of central socioeconomic planning. Bull Int Stat Inst 46:511–522
Zagórski K (1994) Hope factor, inequality, and legitimacy of systemic transformations: the case of Poland. Communis Post-Commun 27(4):357–376
Zagórski K, Evans MD, Kelley J, Piotrowska K (2014) Does national income inequality affect individuals' quality of life in Europe? Inequality, happiness, finances, and health. Soc Indic Res 117(3):1089–1110
Zapf W (2000) Social reporting in the 1970s and in the 1990s. Soc Indic Res 51(1):1–15

About the Authors

Andrzej K. Koźmiński is a member of Polish Academy of Sciences, International Academy of Management, and European Academy, holding multiple titles of doctor honoris causa at such prestigious universities as ESCP Paris among others. He serves as the President of Koźmiński University, Warsaw, Poland teaches there and used to teach at various American and European universities. Professor Koźmiński has distinguished himself in combining theoretical and empirical work in economics, sociology, and management science. He has published more than 450 books, articles, and chapters of coauthored books in Polish, English, and French.

Adam Noga is a specialist in business cycles and enterprises, competition, accounting theories and macroeconomics. Currently, he lectures at Kozminski University in Warsaw. Professor Noga has received in 1994 the Prize of Bank Handlowy for his book "Domination and effective competition". In 2009, he has received an award for the best book on the enterprise "Theories of the Firms" presenting his "theory of confirm". In 2013, in the publication "The state as a leverage of household revenues", he has presented another original theory of a "constant state" in economy.

Katarzyna Piotrowska works at Kozminski University where she is a faculty member in Departments of Quantitative Methods and Information Technology. She teaches statistics and social research methodology. Among her main academic engagements and interests are the psychology of decision making – especially in the field of people's reactions after making decisions, socio-economic development as well as economic attitudes and behaviour. She is also engaged in projects from other fields including management and medicine.

A. K. Koźmiński et al., *The Balanced Development Index for Europe's OECD Countries, 1999–2017*, SpringerBriefs in Economics,
https://doi.org/10.1007/978-3-030-39240-6

Krzysztof Zagórski teaches sociology and serves as a director of Empirical Sociology Center at Kozminski University, Warsaw. He has authored and co-authored about 150 publications (books, chapters and articles) devoted mainly to social stratification and mobility, public opinion and attitudes, social statistics and social indicators, economic and political sociology as well as living conditions and satisfactions. His current academic interests include socio-economic development, living conditions and economic attitudes.